# STUART BLAND

# GRAPH|CAL COMMUN|CATION

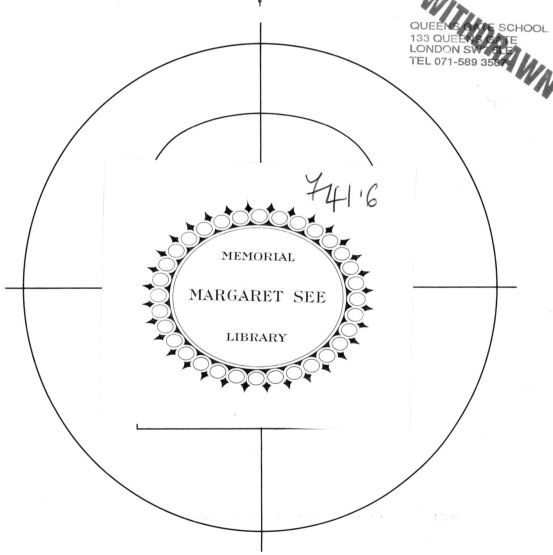

Longman

# Acknowledgements

I wish to thank my colleagues and the pupils at Ewell Castle School.

We are grateful to the following for permission to reproduce photographs:

Automobile Association, page 38 (top); The Bluebell Railway, page 48; British Rail, page 42; British Telecom, page 52; London Transport, pages 39, 40, 41 and 42; Sealink, page 6.

Ordnance Survey maps are reproduced with the permission of the controller of Her Majesty's Stationery Office, crown copyright reserved, pages 37 (top) RAC map, 43 and 44.

LONGMAN GROUP UK LIMITED
Longman House, Burnt Mill, Harlow, Essex CM20 2JE, England
and Associated Companies throughout the world.

First published 1986
Seventh impression 1993
ISBN 0 582 22445 4

Set in Linotron Rockwell

Produced by Longman Singapore Publishers Pte Ltd
Printed in Singapore

The publisher's policy is to use paper manufactured from
sustainable forests.

# Contents

QUEENS GATE SCHOOL
133 QUEENS GATE
LONDON SW7 5LE
TEL 071-589 3587

# Introduction

The importance of graphicacy, or the ability to communicate by means of drawings and diagrams, is widely recognised in today's world of technology—more so in that it crosses language barriers and provides us with a single system that can be universally understood. Perhaps it is not surprising therefore that syllabus changes over recent years have reflected the wider significance of graphical communication to the world at large.

The new graphical communication syllabuses relate orthographic projection to a much wider variety of objects than simply engineering parts. The approach in this two-book course therefore is to relate drawings to everyday objects (modern and traditional) and to involve the student in the problem-solving and design aspects of graphical work. To this end the various methods of pictorial representation have been dealt with in detail, with particular emphasis on buildings and workshop tools. The design approach to a number of the topics will be of particular use to those studying craft, design and technology. Methods of graphical illustration, circuit diagrams and flow charts have been dealt with in great detail to enable the student to appreciate the wide subject area that graphical communication now covers.

*Stuart Bland*

# Note to the teacher

Book 2 covers approximately half the full syllabus. Each chapter deals with a particular topic through to examination level. Chapter 10 on orthographic projection provides a second stage to the initial coverage of this topic in Book 1.

Each chapter is graded in difficulty, so that the teacher can select material suitable for the class or individual group of students. Some of the practice items can be carried out as project work, over a period of time, if preferred.

Methods of shading, colour, ink drawing, the use of stencils and drawing aids should be encouraged, since such methods are all used in modern drawing offices and design studios. However, students should be competent in freehand work before drawing aids are used.

# Review Summary

The following pages are a brief summary of the important topics covered in Book 1.

## Geometrical figures and patterns

Construction of a regular polygon given one side:

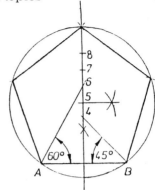

Construction of a regular polygon in a circle:

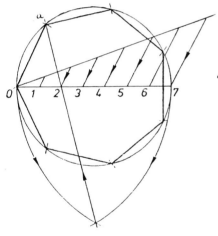

Regular figures:

equilateral triangle · square · pentagon · hexagon

The pattern here is made up of a combination of equilateral triangles.

 PRACTICE 1

Design and draw patterns using some of the geometrical shapes shown above. Use colour and/or ink.

## Arcs joining straight lines

Draw the angle, and to obtain the centre B of the arc, draw construction lines parallel to, and of the required radius away from the angle.

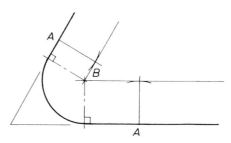

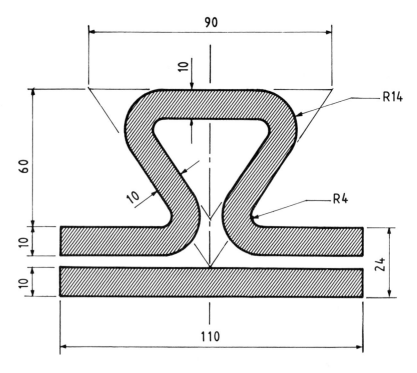

⊕ PRACTICE 2

The letters S and L are formed into a bollard to form the logo for Sealink. Make an accurate copy of this drawing to a scale of full size. All the large arcs are radius 14mm and all the small arcs are radius 4mm. Use coloured pencils or colourwash to colour the logo and the background correctly.

# Tangential arcs

For arcs which are tangential to circles, the centres of the arcs are constructed and calculated from the centres of the circles and arcs.

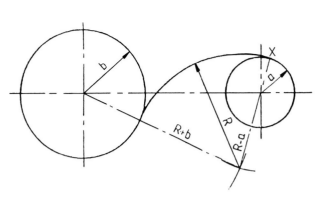

PRACTICE

To a scale of 1½ times full size make an accurate drawing of the cable car. Use shading on your drawing.

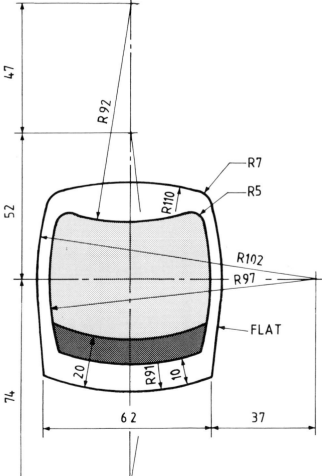

# Symbols and logotypes

## Pictograms

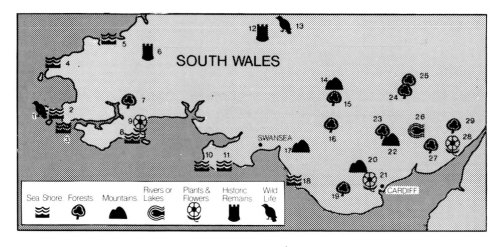

Symbols, usually in the form of a picture in silhouette, are used to convey information easily.

The example is part of a tourist guide for South Wales and symbols have been used to indicate the various places of interest.

**⊕ PRACTICE 1**

Make a list of the various different uses of pictograms, eg. road sign etc.

## Logograms

Logograms are used for company signs and symbols.

The photograph shows the logo for Woolworth. The letters W and O of Woolworth are formed into a logo.

**⊕ PRACTICE 2**

List four companies that use the initial letters of their name to form a logo. Sketch and colour two of them.

Other logograms use a picture which is related to the function of the company. In this example a silhouette of a fan is used. Xpelair manufacture fans. (The fan also forms a letter X).

**⊕ PRACTICE 3**

Name and sketch the logo of three other firms that use a picture as part of the logo. Use colour and shading.

# Constructions for the ellipse

⊕ **PRACTICE 1** ──────

Construct ellipses given that the major axis is 120mm and the minor axis is 70mm:

1. Using the auxiliary circle method.
2. Using the radial line method.

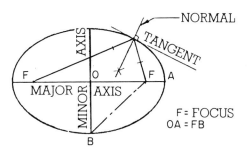

▲ Parts of the ellipse.

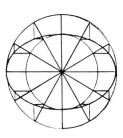

▲ Auxiliary circle method.

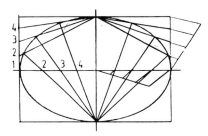

▲ Radial line method.

# Statistical charts

The two examples are three dimensional pie charts. Three dimensional charts are becoming more common and visually, they tend to have more impact than 'flat' two dimensional charts.

In the second chart a portion has been removed for emphasis.

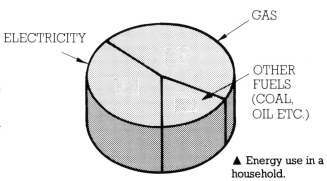

▲ Energy use in a household.

KEY

☐ HOME

▨ SCHOOL

▲ Where I spent my time yesterday.

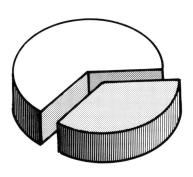

⊕ **PRACTICE 1** ──────

Draw a pie chart similar to the one here to illustrate where you spent your time last Saturday. Use colour. An isometric circle or ellipse template can be used for drawing the ellipses here.

## Freehand sketching

The drawings show the stages for sketching a firmer chisel in isometric projection.

Some of the construction lines have been omitted on some of the drawings for the purpose of clarity.

## Orthographic projection

The drawing is based on the cassette player in the photograph.

⊕ PRACTICE 1

Draw a plan, front elevation and end elevation to a scale of full size. Only the important dimensions are given and you should use your own judgement where they are missing. The drawings show how you should position your views.

⊕ PRACTICE 2

By means of freehand sketches design:

1. A method of attaching a shoulder strap to the player.
2. A fixture on the back of the player to enable it to be secured to an inside pocket of a jacket.

⊕ PRACTICE

Make a freehand sketch of a mortice chisel.

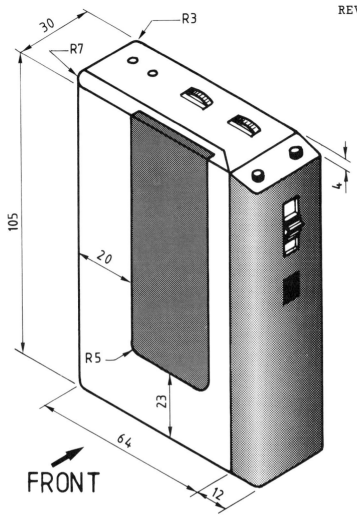

30

R3

R7

105

20

R5

23

64

12

4

▼ The position of
the views and the
symbol for first
angle projection.

FRONT

▼ The position of
the views and the
symbol for third
angle projection.

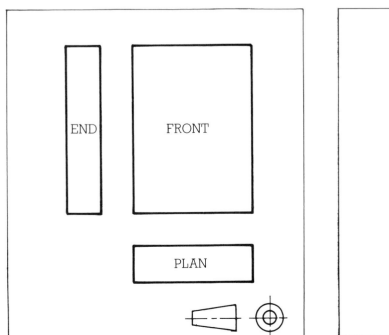

END

FRONT

PLAN

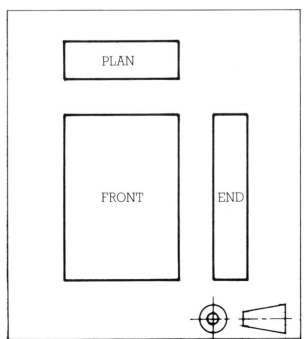

PLAN

FRONT

END

## Axonometric projection

In very simple terms the following rules apply to axonometric drawings.

> 1. Lines representing height are vertical.
> 2. Sides are sloping and edges are parallel.

Various examples are shown below.

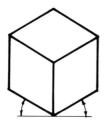

▲ Isometric: sides angled at 30°.

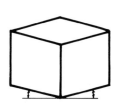

▲ Dimetric: both sides angled the same, but not 30°. (15° in this example.)

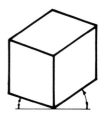

▲ Trimetric: sides angled differently.

## Oblique projection

The front is the true shape and the side and top are angled at 45° or 30°:

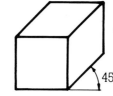

◄ Cavalier oblique: true length for sloping sides.

45°

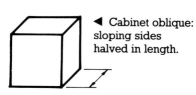

◄ Cabinet oblique: sloping sides halved in length.

## Planometric projection

Top and bottom are true shape and angled at 45°, 45° or 30°, 60°.

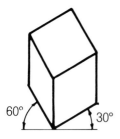

60°  30°

## Perspective

Sides converge to one or more vanishing points, (VP).

*Note:* Isometric and oblique projection are dealt with in detail in Book 1.

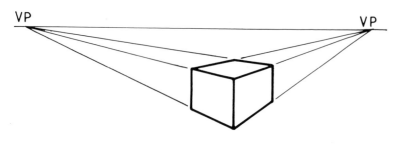

VP        VP

## Perspective drawing

Drawings in perspective are more life-like than those in isometric, oblique or planometric. The sides of objects appear to converge to a point or points in the distance. These points are referred to as vanishing points (VP).

1. The photograph shows a canal whose sides converge to a vanishing point on the horizon.

2. Distances become progressively shorter as the vanishing point is approached.

   This is shown in the photograph of an office block. The distances between the balconies become shorter.

3. The position of the observer will determine the position of the vanishing points.

◀ Observer high.

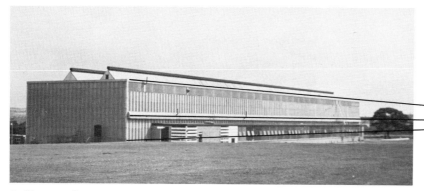

▲ Observer low.

## Single point perspective

All edges converge to a single vanishing point.

The photograph of a garage block shows one vanishing point, because only one side of the building is seen. VP

The photograph of an Underground railway station shows a single vanishing point in the tunnel.

In a similar manner this perspective drawing of a room uses a single vanishing point in the centre.

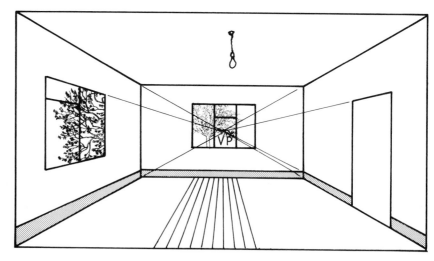

⊕ PRACTICE 1

Sketch your living room at home. Position the vanishing point near the centre of one wall or window. As you approach the vanishing point distances will become shorter.

Single point perspective can be used as an adaptation of oblique projection. If so, these rules apply:

1. The front of the object is drawn to its true shape.
2. The sides and top converge to the vanishing point as illustrated in the examples below.

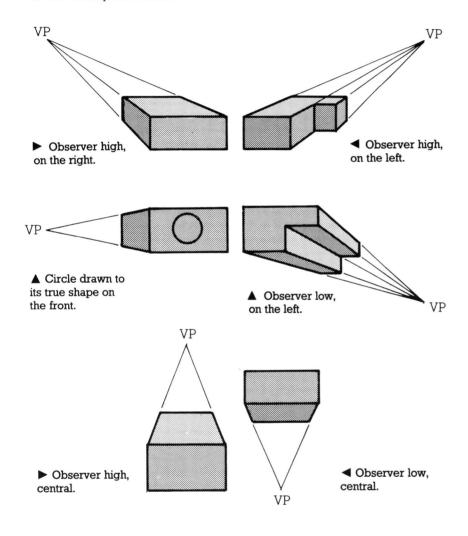

VP

▶ Observer high,
on the right.

VP

◀ Observer high,
on the left.

VP

▲ Circle drawn to
its true shape on
the front.

▲ Observer low,
on the left.

VP

VP

▶ Observer high,
central.

VP

◀ Observer low,
central.

## PRACTICE 2

For the top four drawings,
sketch each block several times
with the vanishing points in
different positions. Use your
own measurements and add
colour or shading.

## Two point perspective

The two sides converge to vanishing points. The vanishing points lie on the same horizontal line, and in practice are spaced at great distance from the object. Measurements for height are taken from the nearest corner of the object.

VP          VP

◄ Vanishing points are almost central with the building, and the roof is not seen.

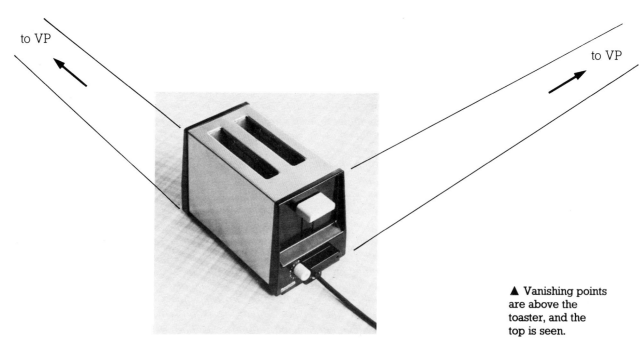

to VP

to VP

▲ Vanishing points are above the toaster, and the top is seen.

The three examples below show how simple objects are drawn in two point perspective.

**PRACTICE 3** ——————————————————

Using your own measurements draw each object three times:

1. With the vanishing points high.
2. Slightly above the object.
3. Below the object.

Position your drawing off centre in each case. Use colour or shading.

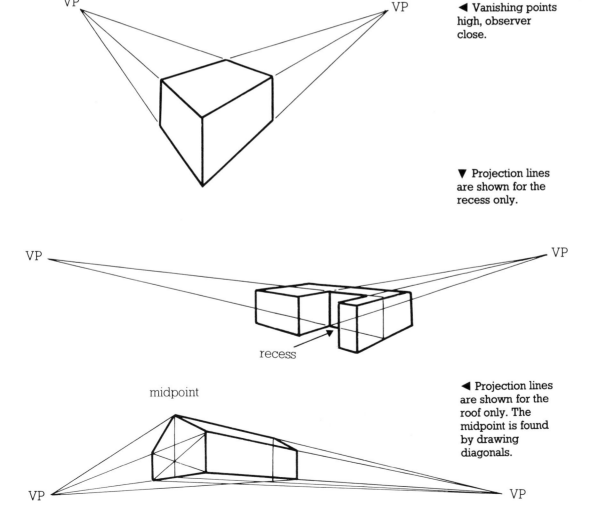

◄ Vanishing points high, observer close.

▼ Projection lines are shown for the recess only.

VP                                                          VP

recess

midpoint

◄ Projection lines are shown for the roof only. The midpoint is found by drawing diagonals.

VP                                                          VP

## Three point perspective

A third vanishing point is used in this drawing to give an impression height. The drawing becomes rather distorted in shape.

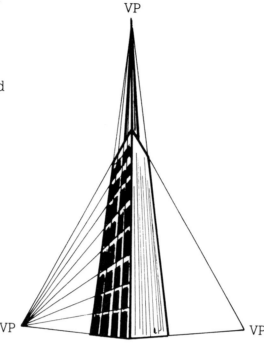

## Estimated perspective

Orthographic views of a block are shown below. In the perspective view, the sides have been shortened in such a way as to produce correct proportions. For estimated drawings you should use your own judgement for lengths.

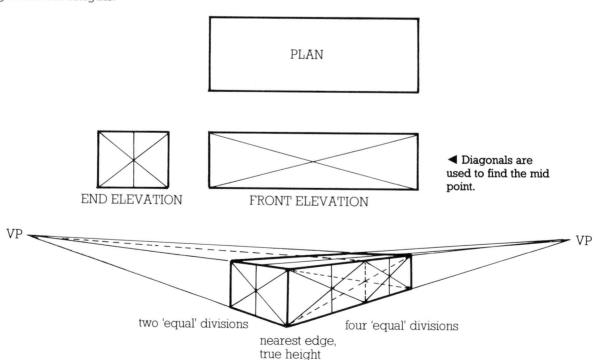

PLAN

END ELEVATION    FRONT ELEVATION

◀ Diagonals are used to find the mid point.

two 'equal' divisions    four 'equal' divisions

nearest edge,
true height

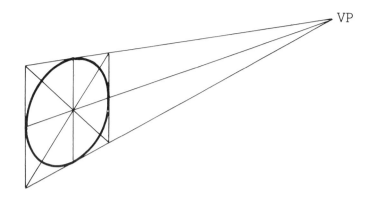

**PRACTICE 4**

The circle is seen as a distorted ellipse in perspective drawings.

Sketch the ellipse inside a 'square' as shown. Note how lengths are foreshortened in this 'square'.

To save time, where accuracy is not too important, distances for perspective drawings and sketches are estimated.

1. The height of the nearest corner will be the true height.

2. The lengths of the sides will be foreshortened. The nearer the vanishing point the shorter the side will be.

3. 'Mid points' can be found by drawing diagonals.

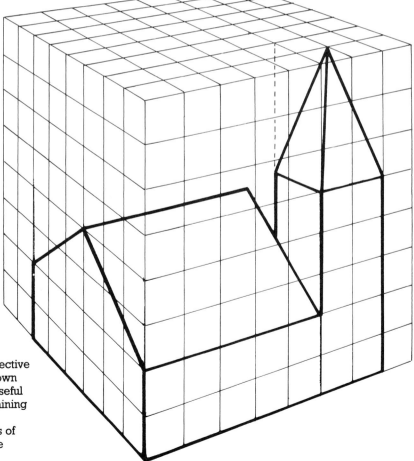

► A perspective grid, as shown here, is a useful aid for obtaining the correct proportions of perspective drawings.

## Measured point perspective

The following drawings show the procedure for making an accurate two point perspective drawing of a building. All the measurements given are in metres and the drawing is produced using a suitable scale.

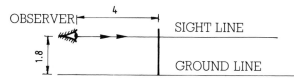

1. Draw in the ground line, mark the sight line. This will be determined by the height of the observer above the ground.
2. Draw a plan of the building showing the position from which its nearest edge or corner is viewed. Mark the position of the observer (in this case 4 metres from the corner).

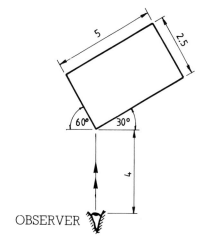

3. The ground line, sight line and the nearest edge of the building are shown drawn to scale.

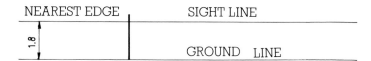

4. Position the observer, drawn to scale, from the nearest corner. Draw in lines to represent the two sides shown on the plan. Mark the vanishing points VP1 and VP2.

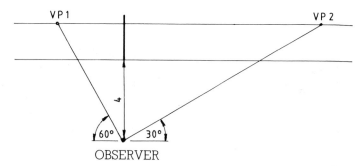

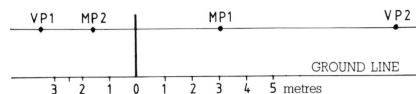

5. To obtain the measuring points, MP1 and MP2, place your compass on VP1 and VP2 and strike arcs respectively from the observer.

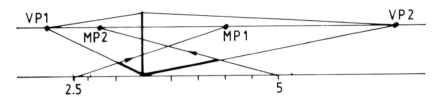

6. On the ground line mark the scale in metres.

7. To obtain the lengths of the two sides in the perspective drawing, draw lines from the scale to the measuring points.

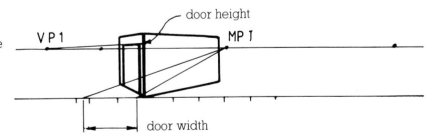

8. Draw in the outline.

9. The widths of doors etc. on the sides are marked off from the measuring points in a similar way.

**PRACTICE 5**

Make a copy of this drawing using the given measurements.

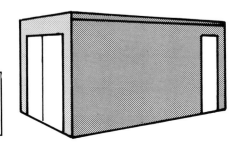

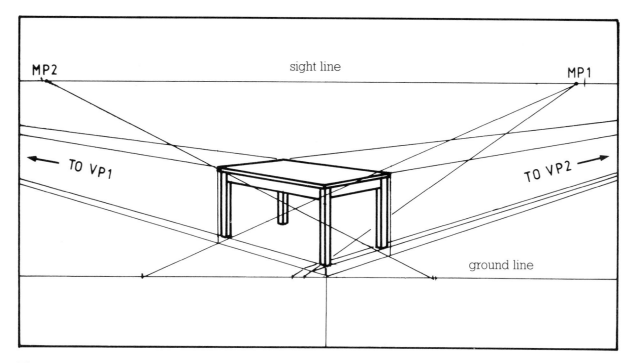

The perspective drawing of a kitchen table shows the vanishing points and the position of the observer outside the edge of the paper. For most drawings this will be the case and the vanishing points should be located on the drawing board as shown in the photograph.

## PRACTICE 6

Make a copy of this drawing, given the following information:

| TOP | 1800mm long 600mm wide 50mm thick |
|---|---|
| LEGS | 700mm long 70mm square |
| RAILS | 75mm wide |

The top overlaps the frame and legs by 75mm on all sides.

The table is angled at 30°, 60° to the observer who is 1.8m tall and is 4.5m from the nearest edge.

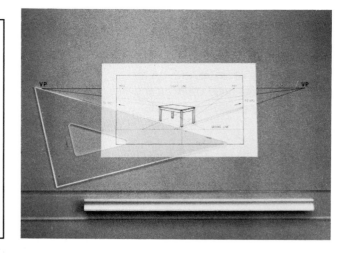

## PRACTICE 7

The drawing shows two orthographic views of a piece of square tube. Sketch or draw the following views ensuring that the hole can be clearly seen in each view. All vanishing points and horizons should be indicated.

1. A one-point perspective view.
2. A two-point perspective view.
3. A three-point perspective view.     *(Cambridge (adapted), 1983)*

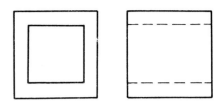

## PRACTICE 8

Two views of a bungalow are given in which the principal dimensions only are shown, in metres.

Working to scale 1:100, make an estimated perspective drawing of the bungalow suitable for inclusion in a house agent's brochure.

Hidden detail is not required.
Colouring and/or shading can be used.     *(London, June 1983)*

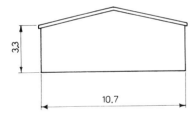
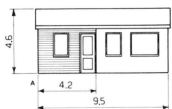

All dimensions in metres

## PRACTICE 9

Complete, within a two point perspective grid, a perspective view of the model aeroplane shown in the orthographic views below. One square of the perspective grid represents one square of the orthographic grid on which the views of the aeroplane have been drawn.

Show the thickness of the wings and tail as single lines. You may approximate the shape of the windows.

*(Cambridge (adapted), 1982)*

(Use tracing paper to copy the grid on page 19, and add extra lines if necessary.)

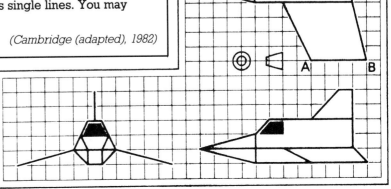

# Planometric drawing

Planometric drawings are used by architects and room planners to show the interiors of buildings.

---

**The following rules apply to planometric drawings:**
1. The plan is drawn to its true shape but it is angled at 45° and 45° or 30° and 60° to the horizontal.
2. Heights are shown to be their true length.

---

The drawings below show the stages for making a planometric drawing of a block and cylinder.

1. Draw the plan angled at 45° in this case.

2. Draw in the sides and complete the block. Draw in the base of the cylinder (a true circle in the plan).

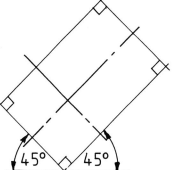

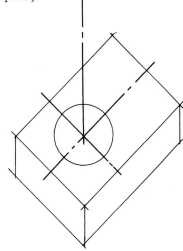

3. Draw in the vertical centre line, mark the height, draw in the top of the cylinder and the sides.

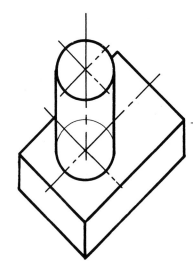

---

**PRACTICE 1**

Make a copy of this drawing using the following measurements:
BOX: length 80mm, width 50mm, height 20mm.
CYLINDER: ⌀ 25mm, height 60mm.

## How to make a planometric drawing of a room

The drawings show the plan and elevation of a room in a house.
Measurements for the planometric view are taken from this drawing.

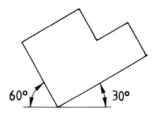

ELEVATION

PLAN

1. Draw the plan, in this example angled at 30°, 60°.

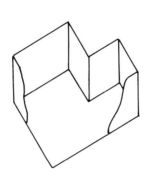

60°          30°

2. Draw the walls to form a box.

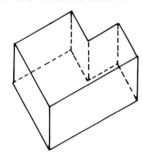

3. The front walls are cut away to show details of the inside.

4. Add the thickness to the walls.

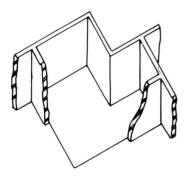

5. Complete the drawing by adding details of the window and the door. Note the use of a compass arc for the position of the open door.

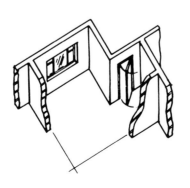

**PRACTICE 2**

To a suitable scale, make a planometric drawing of the living room in your home. Show the doors and windows and position your drawing to show the greatest amount of detail.

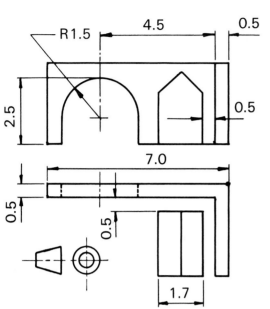

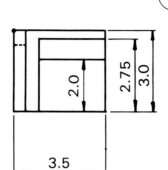

## PRACTICE 3

Three views of a film set are shown here. The set consists of a walled garden corner, arched entrance and a garden shed.

Using a scale 1:50 prepare a planometric view of the set. All dimensions are in metres.

*(AEB, 1983)*

## PRACTICE 4

A cut-away illustration of a lighthouse is required for a children's magazine. Details of the lighthouse, which is circular in section except for the base, are given on the right.

Draw scale 1:100 in planometric projection, 45°/45°, a view of one half of the lighthouse as indicated in the small sketch. The roof, lamproom and gallery may be drawn using single lines; the thickness of the walls of the tower must be included.

Do not include the shading of the glass of the lamproom, door or windows, although you should shade the 'cut' surface of the tower.

All dimensions are in metres.

*(London, June 1984)*

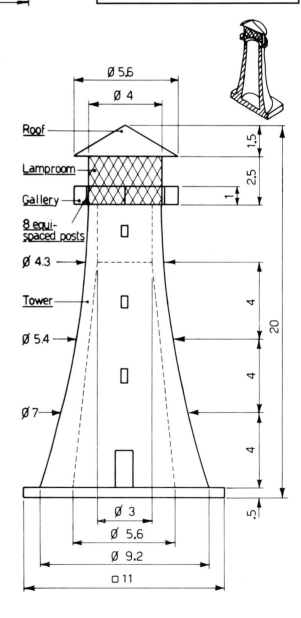

## Graphical symbols (1) and scale recommendations

These are based on British Standards Institute publication BS 1192,
*Building Drawing Practice.*

### Selected symbols for building plans

north point

new trees

existing trees

existing trees removed

### Services (piped and ducted)

discharge pipe
D P

drainpipe

gulley
G

manhole (soil)
M H

manhole (surface water)
M H

vent pipe
V P

### Water supply

cold water cistern
C W C

cold water storage tank
C W T

draining tap
D T

gas water heater
G W H

header feed and
expansion tank
F & EXPT

hot or cold water draw off

hot water cylinder
H W C

stop valve

## Block plan

A block plan shows roads, outlines of buildings and site boundaries.

The drawing shows an example of a block plan drawn to a scale of 1:1250.

The site which has been outlined with the building shaded will be shown in the more detailed drawings on the following pages.

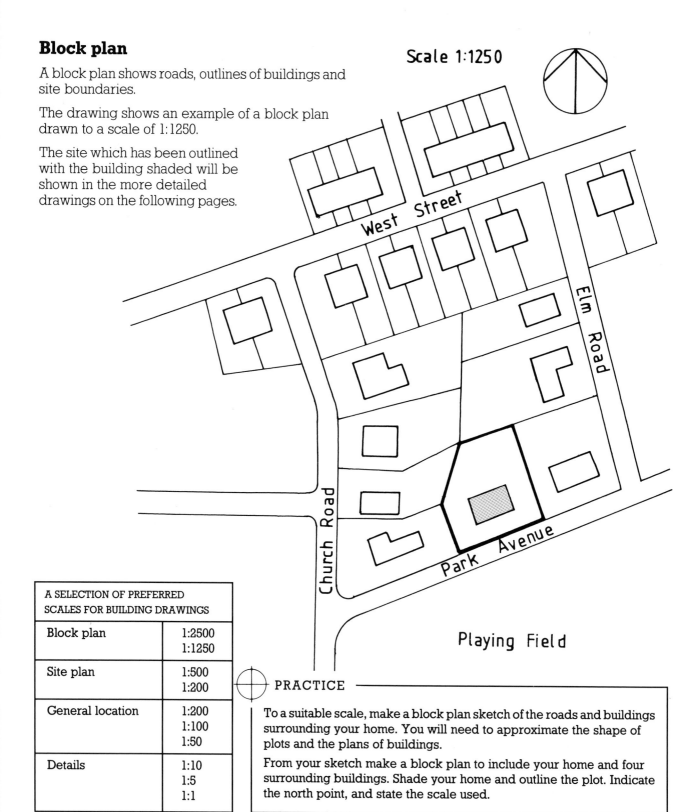

Scale 1:1250

| A SELECTION OF PREFERRED SCALES FOR BUILDING DRAWINGS | |
|---|---|
| Block plan | 1:2500<br>1:1250 |
| Site plan | 1:500<br>1:200 |
| General location | 1:200<br>1:100<br>1:50 |
| Details | 1:10<br>1:5<br>1:1 |

PRACTICE

To a suitable scale, make a block plan sketch of the roads and buildings surrounding your home. You will need to approximate the shape of plots and the plans of buildings.

From your sketch make a block plan to include your home and four surrounding buildings. Shade your home and outline the plot. Indicate the north point, and state the scale used.

## Site plan

The drawing is an example of a site plan showing the plot which was outlined on the block plan on the previous page. Note the following features:

1. The buildings are shown as outlines and boundaries are marked.
2. The scale and north point are indicated.
3. Waste pipe runs, manholes and trees are indicated.
4. Important dimensions are marked in metres.
5. The site is numbered.

SCALE 1:500

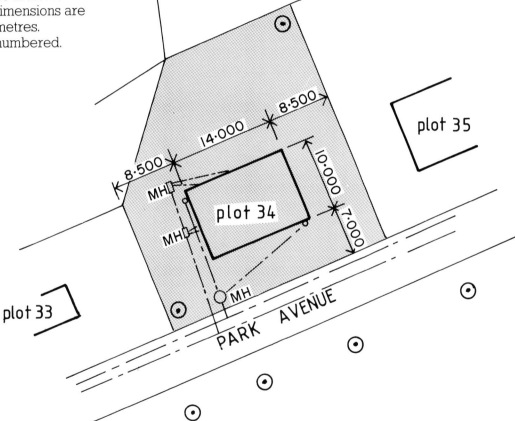

PRACTICE

On a sheet of A3 paper, draw a site plan, scale 1:500 of your area. The plan should include your home and the surrounding buildings and should fill the paper.

Your home and plot should be outlined and shaded, indicate any trees and name the roads.

You will need to make rough sketches and it will be necessary to approximate the size and shape of the surrounding plots and buildings.

## Location drawing

In this example of a location drawing, the plan of the ground floor of a building shows the positions of the rooms, doors, windows, and wall thickness. Other details such as drains could be shown but have been omitted in this case.

SCALE 1:100

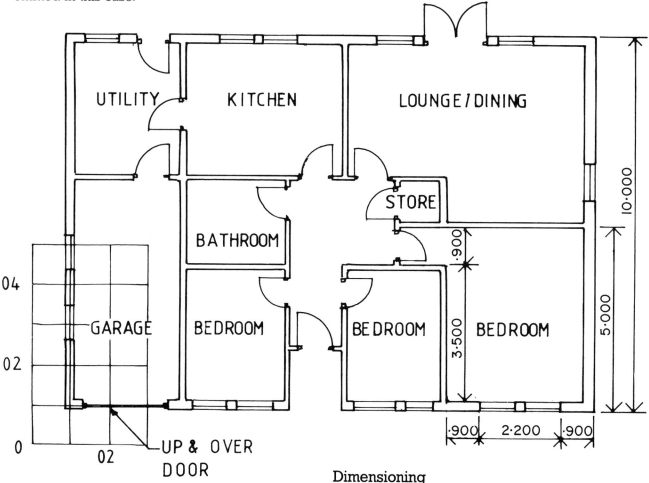

### Dimensioning

1. By grid:
   An example of a grid is shown on the left hand part of the drawing. The grid size will depend on the scale of the drawing. In this case each square represents 1000mm.
2. By arrows:
   An example of dimensioning by arrows is shown on the right hand side of the drawing. Measurements are shown in metres.

*Note:* Dimensioning methods on the drawing should be consistent and NOT a mixture as shown here.

---

⊕ PRACTICE

To a scale of 1:50 make an accurate drawing of the bedroom shown in the bottom right hand corner of the drawing. Interior walls are 125 thick and exterior walls are 300 thick.

Dimension your drawing by means of a grid.

## Building plans: the basic procedure

The drawings show the procedure for producing plans for a house extension.

1. The freehand drawing shows the house viewed from the back and the position of the proposed garage.

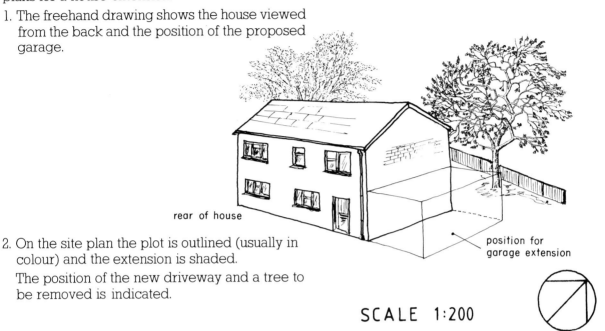

rear of house

position for garage extension

2. On the site plan the plot is outlined (usually in colour) and the extension is shaded.

   The position of the new driveway and a tree to be removed is indicated.

SCALE 1:200

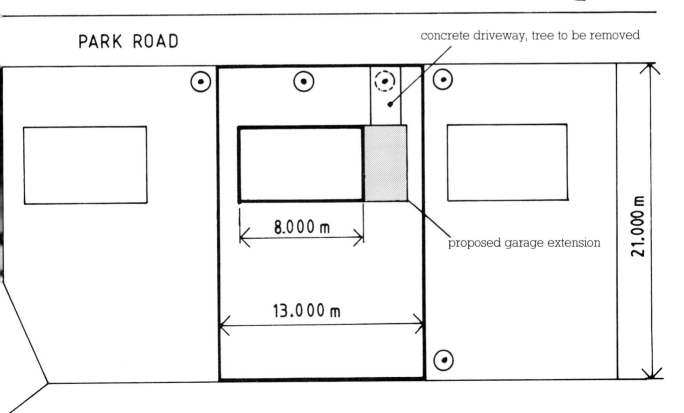

PARK ROAD

concrete driveway, tree to be removed

8.000 m

13.000 m

proposed garage extension

21.000 m

3. The location drawing is drawn to a larger scale to show more detail. Shading has been used to emphasise the extent of the building.

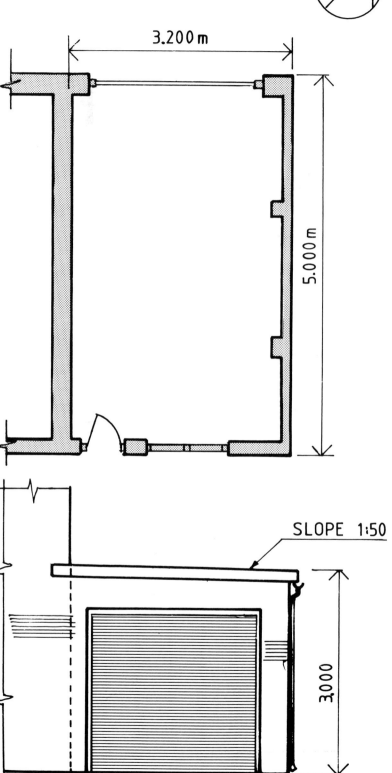

SCALE 1:50

3.200 m

5.000 m

PLAN

SLOPE 1:50

NORTH WEST
ELEVATION

3000

## Graphical symbols (2)

The selected heating and ventilation symbols are based on BS 1192, *Building Drawing Practice.*

A scale of 1:50 is used for most building drawings where general details are shown.

For complex installations, separate drawings of the different services are produced.

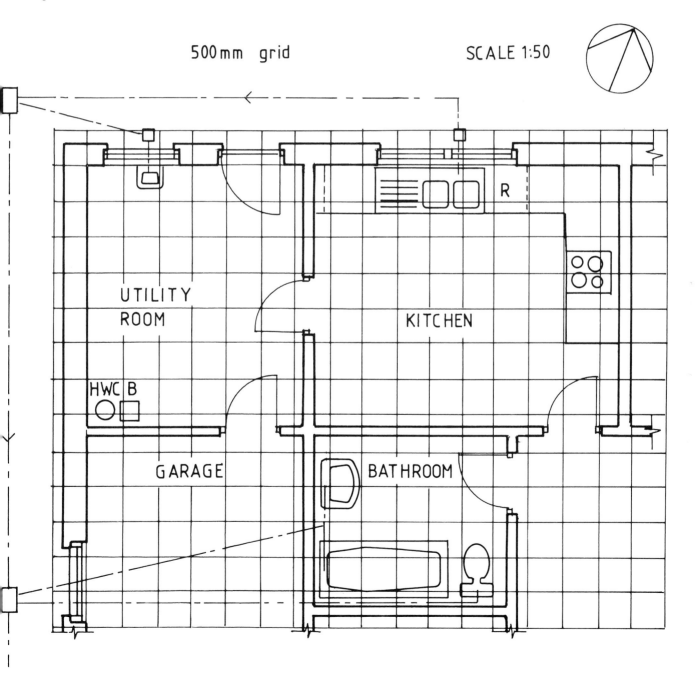

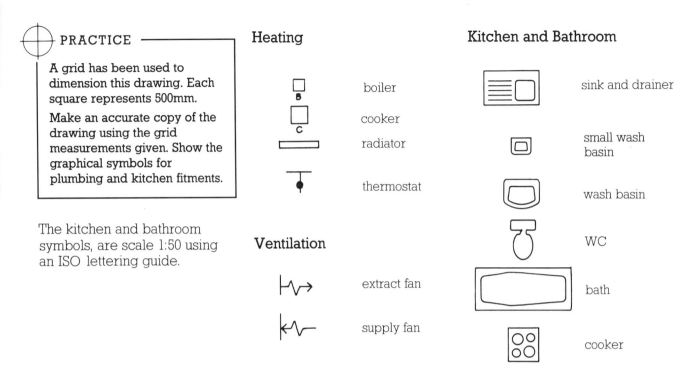

PRACTICE

A grid has been used to dimension this drawing. Each square represents 500mm.

Make an accurate copy of the drawing using the grid measurements given. Show the graphical symbols for plumbing and kitchen fitments.

The kitchen and bathroom symbols, are scale 1:50 using an ISO lettering guide.

**Heating**

boiler

cooker

radiator

thermostat

**Ventilation**

extract fan

supply fan

**Kitchen and Bathroom**

sink and drainer

small wash basin

wash basin

WC

bath

cooker

# Graphical symbols (3)

Based on British Standard Institute publication BS 1192, *Building Drawing Practice.*

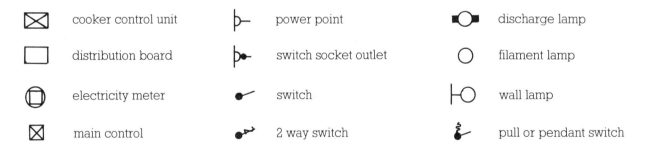

cooker control unit

distribution board

electricity meter

main control

power point

switch socket outlet

switch

2 way switch

discharge lamp

filament lamp

wall lamp

pull or pendant switch

## Selected symbols for electrical installation

Some of the electrical symbols used on building drawings are shown here. (The electrical symbols used for circuit diagrams are different and should not be confused with those shown here.)

The following drawing shows a typical electrical installation using these symbols. Lines are used to connect switches and lamps.

Dimensioning has been omitted from the drawing for the purpose of clarity. The scale and north point are indicated.

# Electrical installation

SCALE 1:50

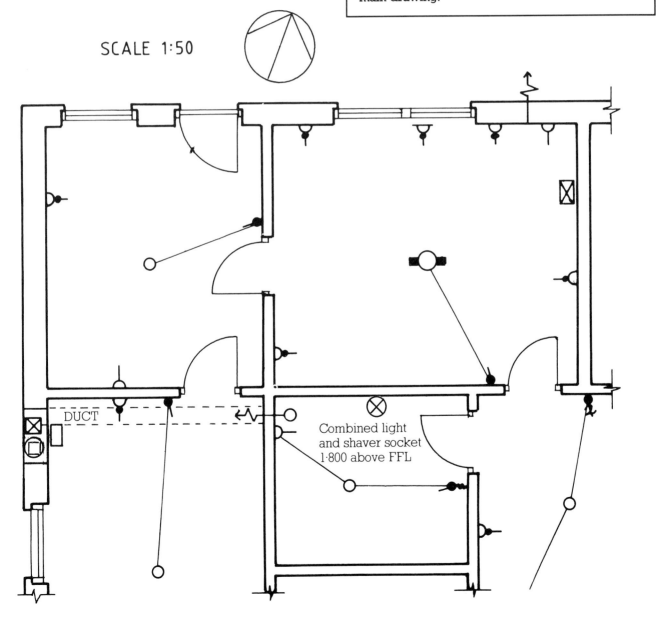

DUCT

Combined light
and shaver socket
1·800 above FFL

## Route maps

The various maps and diagrams show the methods of indicating the route from the railway station to the castle at Farnham.

A is a complete road map of the town. No route is indicated and the user would be expected to sort out the best route.

B shows a simplified geographical map of the best route to be taken. The route can be indicated by a dotted line or colouring. Road junctions are shown to enable the user to locate his position.

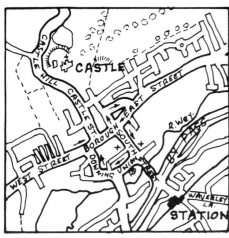

▲ A.    FARNHAM (Centre)

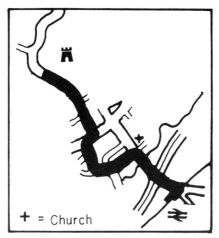

+ = Church

▲ B.

C is a diagrammatic map for a walker. The shortest route has been shown. Junctions and churches are marked and the route is indicated by shading.

D is different to C. A driver would need to use the one-way system through the town centre. The route should be shaded or coloured.

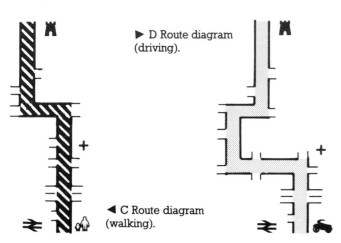

▶ D Route diagram (driving).

◀ C Route diagram (walking).

⊕ PRACTICE 1

Draw a map showing the route from your home to school. The map should be topographical (see page 43) and you should show some of the main features such as bridges, churches, railways etc. Mark your route with a suitable coloured line. Use colour, shading and a key to identify the symbols you have used.

⊕ PRACTICE 2

Simplify the map in *Practice 1* to show your route as a line diagram. This need not be drawn to scale. Colour and a key should be used.

# Town centres

This map of Derby, from a Royal Automobile Club handbook, illustrates one method of showing the routes through and around the centre of the city.

The routes are shown as heavy outlines and arrows are used to indicate one-way systems. Other roads are shown to enable a driver visualise a complete layout of the city.

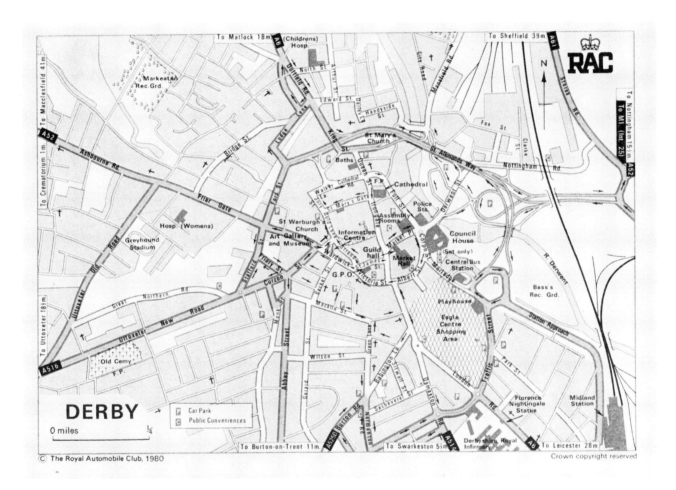

© The Royal Automobile Club, 1980

 PRACTICE 3

Draw a map or diagram to show the best route through or around your nearest large town. Colour can be used and a key may be necessary. Topographical features can be added if they will make your diagram clearer.

## Motorways

Part of a motorway map from an Automobile Association Handbook is shown here.

The map on the far right is geographical. The diagrammatic map next to it shows the motorway only, drawn as a straight vertical line. Junctions are numbered and various symbols are used to indicate routes and service areas. The diagram is uncluttered and colour (not shown here) is used to make the diagram clearer.

Note the use of a key or legend to identify the symbols.

### PRACTICE 4

For a section of motorway nearest to your home, design and draw a route map similar to the AA map shown. Use colour, and invent your own symbols. Indicate a suitable key.

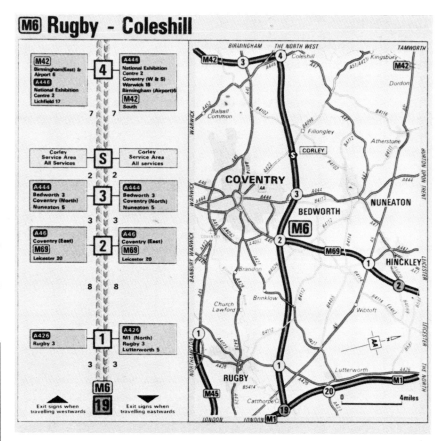

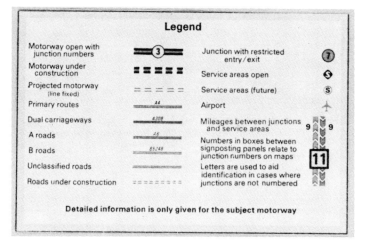

# Network maps

## London Transport

Here are two examples of a
London Underground map.

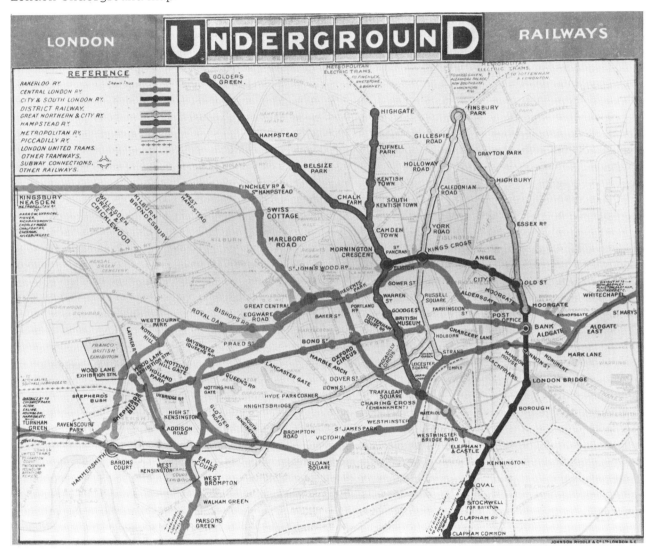

The earlier map, shown above, is
geographical in layout and the
various routes are identified by
colour (not shown here).

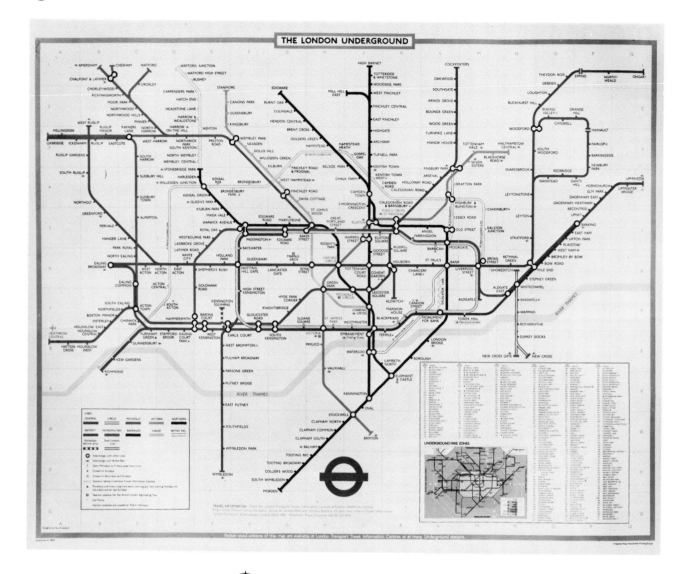

THE LONDON UNDERGROUND

The present day map, shown above, is diagrammatic in layout. Note the use of vertical, horizontal and diagonal lines. Corners have been rounded to give a clearer shape to the diagram.

Colour (not shown here) is used for the different routes. Circles are used to indicate interchange stations and a spur is used to indicate an ordinary station.

In both cases a key is drawn to identify each route.

## PRACTICE 5

Using instruments and colour or ink, make a copy of part of the circle line shown on the map.

## PRACTICE 6

Draw a diagram showing the different bus routes in your area. The routes should be shown as coloured or shaded lines and a key should be used for identification.

# Inter-terminal links by London Underground ⊖

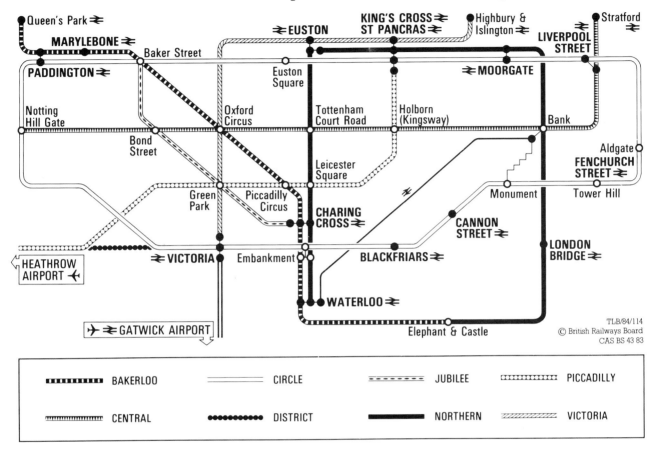

This third diagram is a simplified version of the full London Transport network. It shows how the various mainline railway terminals in London are connected by the Underground system. Different line types have been used to identify the various routes.

The following rules apply to network maps:

1. The route should be drawn by a heavy line.
2. Lines are normally horizontal, vertical or diagonal (45°).
3. Corners are usually rounded.
4. Lines link main centres and unnecessary changes in direction should be avoided.
5. Maps are not drawn to an exact scale.
6. Towns appear in their approximate geographical positions.
7. Some means of indicating a town or station is used. For example a line or circle.
8. Colour will help to identify the different routes and a key should be shown.

## British Rail

The diagram shows the passenger network for Inter-City rail services in Britain.

### Principal Services

⊕ **PRACTICE 7**

On a sheet of A3 paper make a copy of that part of the railway network map which relates to your area.

All diagonal lines are at 45°. Use your own measurements for the length and thickness of the lines. Colour the routes and label the main towns.

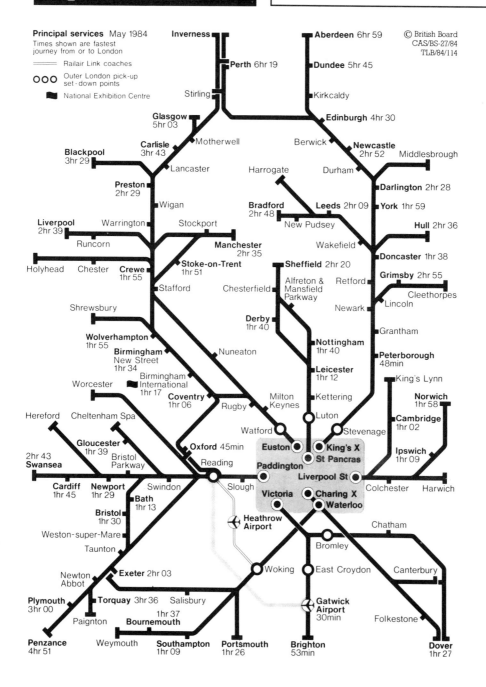

**Principal services** May 1984
Times shown are fastest
journey from or to London

═══ Railair Link coaches

○○○ Outer London pick-up
set-down points

◼ National Exhibition Centre

© British Board
CAS/BS-27/84
TLB/84/114

Inverness
Aberdeen 6hr 59
Perth 6hr 19
Dundee 5hr 45
Stirling
Kirkcaldy
Glasgow 5hr 03
Edinburgh 4hr 30
Carlisle 3hr 43
Motherwell
Berwick
Newcastle 2hr 52
Middlesbrough
Blackpool 3hr 29
Lancaster
Harrogate
Durham
Darlington 2hr 28
Preston 2hr 29
Wigan
Bradford 2hr 48
Leeds 2hr 09
York 1hr 59
Liverpool 2hr 39
Warrington
Stockport
New Pudsey
Hull 2hr 36
Runcorn
Manchester 2hr 35
Wakefield
Holyhead  Chester  Crewe 1hr 55
Stoke-on-Trent 1hr 51
Doncaster 1hr 38
Sheffield 2hr 20
Grimsby 2hr 55
Stafford
Chesterfield
Alfreton & Mansfield Parkway
Retford
Cleethorpes
Shrewsbury
Newark
Lincoln
Derby 1hr 40
Grantham
Wolverhampton 1hr 55
Birmingham New Street 1hr 34
Nuneaton
Nottingham 1hr 40
Peterborough 48min
Worcester
Birmingham International 1hr 17
Leicester 1hr 12
King's Lynn
Coventry 1hr 06
Rugby
Milton Keynes
Kettering
Norwich 1hr 58
Hereford  Cheltenham Spa
Watford
Luton
Stevenage
Cambridge 1hr 02
Gloucester 1hr 39
Oxford 45min
Euston  King's X
Ipswich 1hr 09
2hr 43 Swansea
Bristol Parkway
Reading
St Pancras
Paddington
Liverpool St
Cardiff 1hr 45
Newport 1hr 29
Swindon
Slough
Colchester  Harwich
Bath 1hr 13
Victoria  Charing X
Bristol 1hr 30
Heathrow Airport
Waterloo
Weston-super-Mare
Chatham
Taunton
Bromley
Newton Abbot
Woking
East Croydon
Canterbury
Exeter 2hr 03
Plymouth 3hr 00
Torquay 3hr 36
Salisbury
Gatwick Airport 30min
Paignton
1hr 37
Bournemouth
Folkestone
Penzance 4hr 51
Weymouth
Southampton 1hr 09
Portsmouth 1hr 26
Brighton 53min
Dover 1hr 27

# Ordnance Survey maps

Part of Ordnance Survey sheet No. 178 is shown here.

This is called a topographical map and shows natural features such as hills (contour lines), rivers, rock outcrops and lakes. Man-made features such as roads, bridges, railways and plantations are also shown.

A system of symbols is used to show the various features on the map. The symbols are given in a key, and an example of some of the symbols is shown. Colour enables the various features to be identified more easily (not reproduced here).

A map is drawn to a scale, and in this case the scale is 1:50000. A grid enables places to be easily referenced.

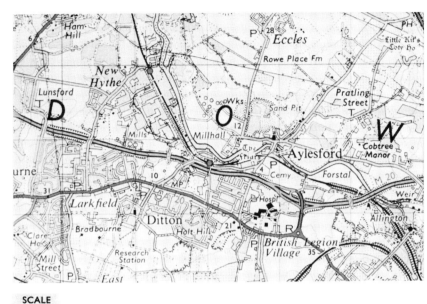

**SCALE**

**1:50 000**

2 centimetres to 1 kilometre (one grid square)

1 kilometre = 0·6214 mile     1 mile = 1·6093 kilometres

## Selected symbols

A selection of Ordnance Survey symbols are shown right:

## Maps for other purposes

Some examples are listed below:

1. Hydrographic maps used by sailors to show tides, currents, ocean depth etc.
2. Tourist maps showing National parks, stately homes and museums.
3. Maps showing camping and caravan sites.
4. Maps for walkers giving details of footpaths.
5. Statistical maps giving information on population, food and mineral production, exports and imports.

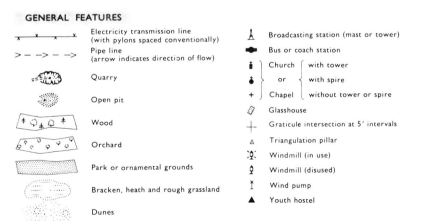

**GENERAL FEATURES**

Electricity transmission line (with pylons spaced conventionally)
Pipe line (arrow indicates direction of flow)
Quarry
Open pit
Wood
Orchard
Park or ornamental grounds
Bracken, heath and rough grassland
Dunes

Broadcasting station (mast or tower)
Bus or coach station
Church { with tower
or { with spire
Chapel { without tower or spire
Glasshouse
Graticule intersection at 5′ intervals
Triangulation pillar
Windmill (in use)
Windmill (disused)
Wind pump
Youth hostel

## Geological maps

The photograph shows part of a geological map which is used to indicate various rock types on the land.

Identification of the rock types is by means of (colour) shading and numbers. A key is used (not shown here) to indicate the meaning of the numbers and shading.

## Historical maps

The photograph shows part of an Ordnance Survey map of the major visible ancient monuments of the British Isles. Various symbols are used to indicate the age of the monument and a key is used to identify each symbol.

Neolithic Age ............................... ○

Bronze Age ................................ ◑

Iron Age .................................... ●

Roman Period ............................. ▫

Post Roman Period ...................... ▦

Uncertain Age ............................. •

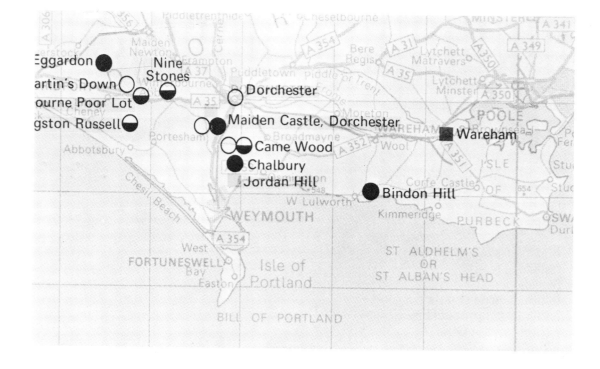

# Weather charts

The drawing shows a simplified version of a weather map. The lines, similar to contour lines, are called isobars and show barometric pressure. Areas of high and low pressure are shown. Fronts and their general movement are indicated by arrows.

More complex weather maps show wind speed, cloud cover, rain and snow, temperature etc. Various symbols are used to show these features.

Notice how weather maps are presented on television and in the daily newspapers.

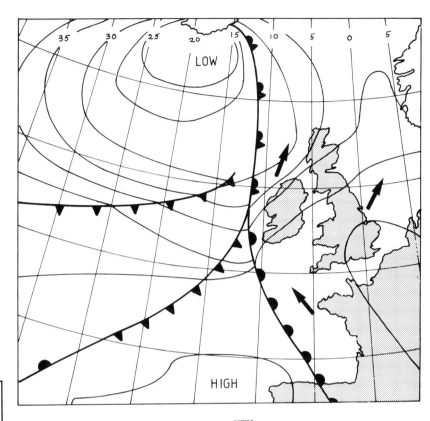

▲ Atlantic weather: noon, February 4.

KEY

— ●— warm front

— ▲— cold front

— ▲●— occluded front

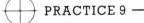

## PRACTICE 8

Draw a map or diagram to show the weather in the British Isles today. Your map should be based on the weather map shown on television or in the local newspaper. Invent your own symbols to indicate rain, sun, cloud, thunderstorms etc. Colour can be used.

## PRACTICE 9

The towns and villages A to N of the island shown on the map, are linked by a series of railway lines.

Design and draw with instruments, a rail map in which stations and lines are shown in a simple geometrical diagram.

A railway traveller should, with the aid of your map, be able to find his way to and from any of the stations A to N on the island.

Colour may be added to your answer if you wish.

*(London, June 1982)*

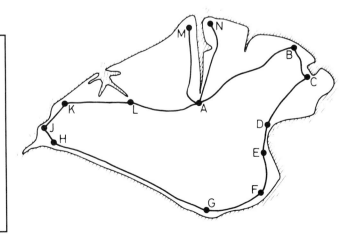

Link mechanisms are the basis for all types of machinery. Various systems are used to convert sliding motion into circular and elliptical motion and vice versa. More complex patterns are built up using a system of levers.

## Levers

The photograph shows bench shears for cutting sheet metal. The system consists of a series of levers arranged to produce considerable force on the blade. The movement of each lever is a simple arc.

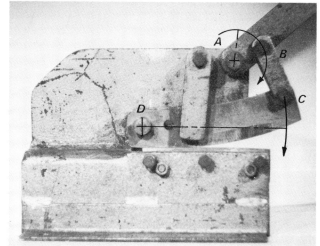

## Procedure

1. A line diagram of the arrangement is drawn to a suitable scale. This drawing shows the system in its open position. The handle AE is much longer than the section shown in the photograph. The joints at A, B, C and D are called pin joints.

   AO = 56
   DO = 38
   DC = 90
   BC = 36
   AB = 20
   AE = 280

2. To determine the movement of the handle, draw the system in its fully open and fully closed positions. Measure distance EE′.

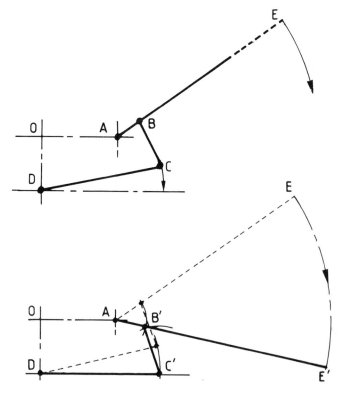

# Link and pivot

The photograph and diagram show an up-and-over garage door in a partly open position.

Pivot A is fixed, pivot B is fixed, rod AB is a link. Pivot C is arranged to slide in the slot.

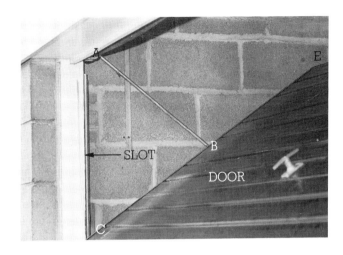

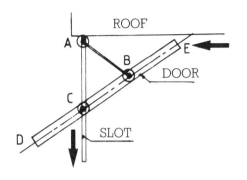

GROUND

## Procedure

1. Draw out the system as a line diagram in the position given.

   AB = BE = BC = CD = 700mm
   AC = 800mm
   Use a scale of 1:20

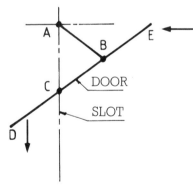

2. Draw the system in other positions, (two such positions are shown). You should draw more to obtain the complete loci of D and E. Trace out the final curves as shown.

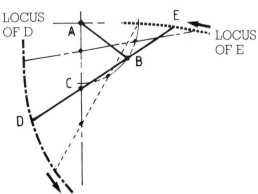

# Piston and crank

The photograph and drawing show the piston and crank mechanism for a steam engine. (A similar arrangement is used on a petrol engine to convert reciprocating motion to circular motion).

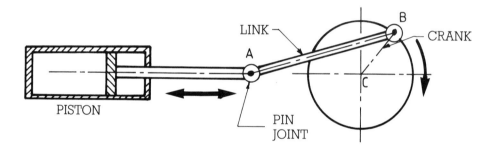

## Procedure

1. Draw out the system as a line drawing using a suitable scale. The piston need not be drawn because point A will always remain on the centre line.

   AB = 110
   BC = 40

   Divide the circle into a convenient number of parts (12 in this case).

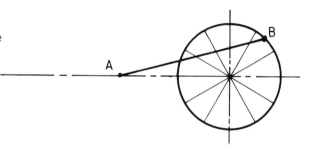

2. Draw out the link arrangement from each point on the circle. The maximum distance moved by the piston is that shown between 9 and 3 on the centre line.

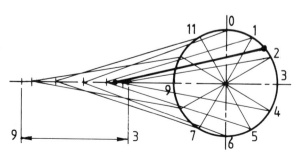

3. The drawing shows the procedure for finding the locus of a point mid way on the link AB. The system is drawn out 12 times and the mid point is marked on each construction line. The points are joined up with a smooth curve.

   Such constructions are useful to determine clearance points on a piece of machinery.

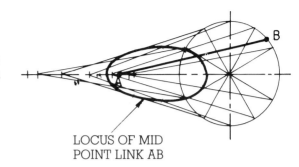

LOCUS OF MID
POINT LINK AB

## Crank and link

The photograph shows part of a power hacksaw machine with the guard removed. The arrangement converts circular motion to reciprocating motion.

For the purpose of this drawing the arrangement has been simplified. The crank BC causes the link BA to move the hacksaw frame along the guide which is pin jointed at C.

### Procedure

1. Draw out the arrangement below (heavy line). For the purpose of this drawing, crank BC revolves in an anti-clockwise direction and A always rests on the horizontal centre line.

   BC = 45mm
   AB = 120mm

   Point A is 25mm above the horizontal centre line through C.
2. Divide the circle into 12 equal parts and draw out the system 12 times. (Three such positions have been shown here).

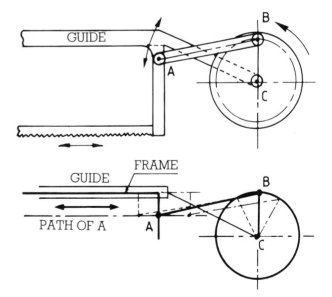

### PRACTICE 1

1. Determine the maximum movement of the hacksaw frame.
2. Construct a locus of the mid-point of AB and design and draw a suitable cover or guard for the crank and part of the link.

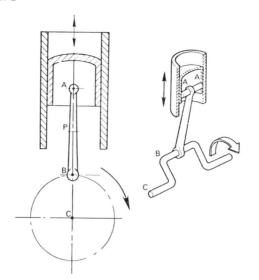

## ⊕ PRACTICE 2

A crank and piston are shown diagrammatically. A, B and C are pin joints. Point A moves to and fro on the vertical axis whilst point B rotates about C. Plot the locus of point P for one revolution.

AP = PB = BC = 30

*(Cambridge (adapted), 1983)*

## ⊕ PRACTICE 3

The rigid link AB has its ends restrained to move in the directions shown along the lines OD and OE respectively.

Plot the locus of point P as the link moves from the vertical to the horizontal position.

OA = OB = 84
AP = 45

*(Cambridge (adapted), 1982)*

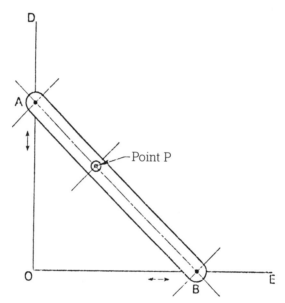

## ⊕ PRACTICE 4

The line diagram shows the principle used in "lazytong" fitting. Some wall telephones are attached in this way so that they can be pulled out to a suitable position and pushed back after use.

Four rods, OB, OD, DE and BF are pinjointed at O, D, B and Y. O is a fixed position. Y is restricted to move along the centre line OG. Plot the positions of F and E from their fully retracted positions to their fully extended positions. Show all constructions.

OD = DY = YF = YE = YB = BO = OY = 50

*(AEB (adapted), June 1982)*

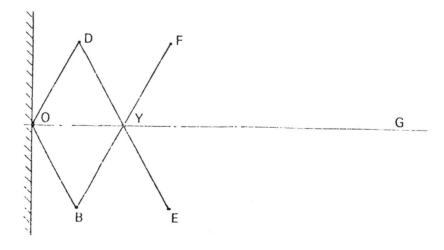

# Ratio of eccentricity

The parabola, ellipse and hyperbola are treated as loci because they all follow definite rules.

The distance from the focus to the curve and the curve to the directrix is always a particular ratio. The constructions below are referred to as the method of 'ratio of eccentricity'.

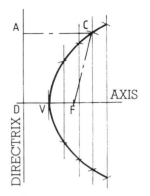

## Parabola

Ratio of eccentricity is always 1:1 or unity.

The vertex (V) is always mid-way between the focus (F) and directrix (D). The vertical construction lines are spaced at convenient points.

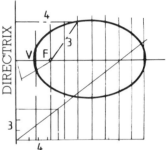

## Ellipse

Ratio of eccentricity is always less than unity. (3:4 in this example.)

The vertex (V) is determined by dividing the distance from the focus to the directrix into the ratio of 3:4.
To determine lengths in the ratio of 3:4 draw the construction shown in the bottom left hand corner and step off lengths for the distance between the focus and the curve.

## Hyperbola

Ratio of eccentricity is always greater than unity. (4:3 in this example.)

The vertex (V) is determined by dividing the distance from the focus to the directrix into the ratio of 4:3.

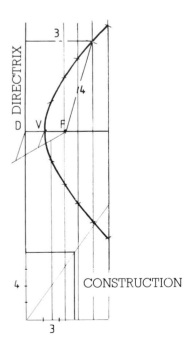

CONSTRUCTION

## Normal and tangent to a parabola:

To draw a normal and tangent at point P, join P to the focus F and construct a right angle. Extend to D on the directrix. A line drawn from D to P will be tangential to the parabola. A normal can be constructed at right angles to the tangent.

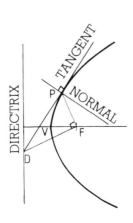

# Parabola and hyperbola

Other methods of construction
*Note:* The construction for the ellipse are shown on p. 9 in *Review Summary.*

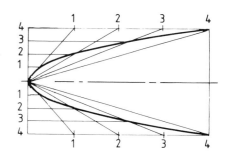

### Parabola in a rectangle:

Make equal divisions as shown. Number the construction lines and follow the numbers to locate points on the parabola.

### Rectangular hyperbola:

Given a point P and the asymptotes, draw lines AP and BP parallel to the asymptotes. Draw radial lines from O. From points C and D draw lines parallel to the asymptotes and repeat for other points.

AP × BP constant. Or for any point on the hyperbola, the horizontal distance from the asymptotex and the vertical distance from an asymptote will always be the same.

The method is the same when the asymptotes are at angles other than 90°

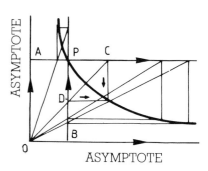

## PRACTICE 1

The photograph shows a radio telescope, the principal section of the bowl of the aerial is a parabola. The bowl has a maximum diameter of 5 metres and the focus of the parabola is 1 metre from its vertex.

Draw the parabola to a scale of 1:20 and insert on your drawing a normal and tangent 1.8 metres from the axis of the parabola.

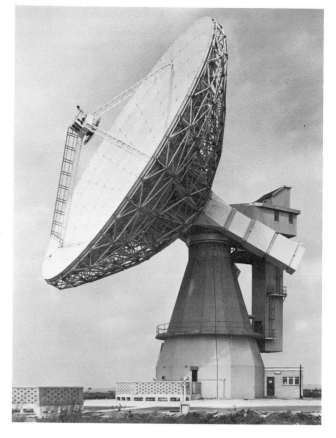

## PRACTICE 2

The photograph shows a sealed beam headlamp for a motor car. The reflector is parabolic in cross-section and the filament of the lamp is at the focus of the reflector. The outside diameter of the reflector is 150mm and the distance from the vertex to the lamp filament is 50mm.

Draw the reflector to a scale of full size.

## PRACTICE 3

The photograph shows the logo for McDonalds, which consists of parabolas drawn as shown.

To a scale of 2 × full size draw the parabolas. These are of the outside of the letter M and you can draw in the inner ones to your own measurements.

Colour in the logo to its correct colour.

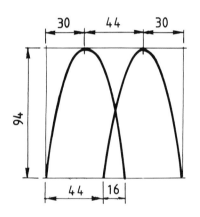

## PRACTICE 4

Draw the cooling tower shown, given that the ratio of eccentricity is 2:1 (hyperbola). The distance from the directrix to the vertex is 18mm.

Draw the right-hand curve first. To obtain the curve on the left, horizontal lines can be drawn and measurements stepped off either side of the centre line (directrix).

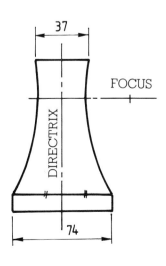

# Other loci

The four drawings show loci based on different rules.

*Involute of a square:*

The involute of a square is the path traced out by the end of a length of string as it is unwound (under tension) from a square (simplified definition).

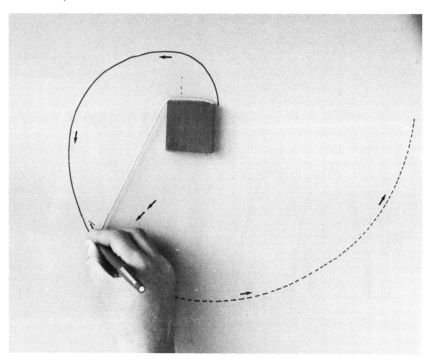

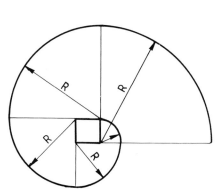

*Involute of a circle:*

The involute of a circle is the path traced out by the end of a length of string as it is unwound (under tension) from a circle (simplified definition).
Involute curves are used to determine the correct shape for inter-meshing gear teeth.
The construction of point 4 on the involute is shown.

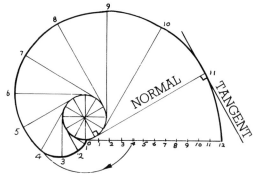

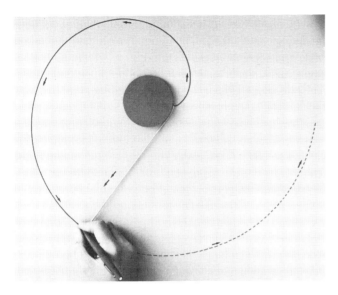

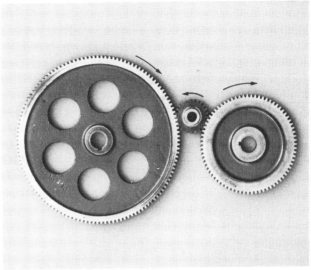

## Archimedean spiral:

The archimedian spiral is the locus of a point as it moves around and away from the centre of a circle at a constant rate. The circle and distance AB are both divided into the same number of equal parts. (In this example 12.)

## Cycloid:

The cycloid is the path traced out by a point on a circle as it rolls along a level surface. Distance AB equals the circumference of the circle and is divided into the same number of equal parts as the circle. (In this example 12 parts.)

▲ The spiral heating element on an electric cooker.

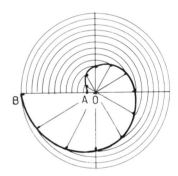

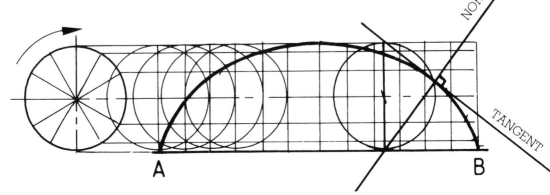

# Helix

The helix is a locus where a point moves along and around a cylinder at a constant rate. Some applications of the helix are shown in the photographs below.

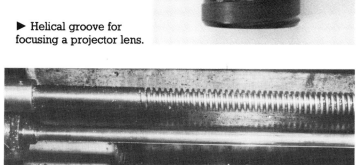

◄ Compression spring.

► Helical groove for focusing a projector lens.

▲ Spiral staircase.

▲ Square thread on a lathe.

PRACTICE 1

Draw each of the following constructions using the measurements given.

*Simple helix:*
Construct using an outside diameter of 75mm and a pitch of 37mm.

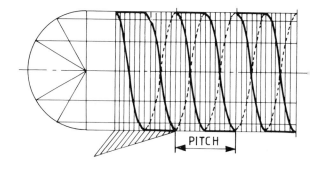

PITCH

*Right-hand square spring:*
Construct using an outside diameter of 75mm and a pitch of 37mm. The thickness of the spring equals half the pitch.

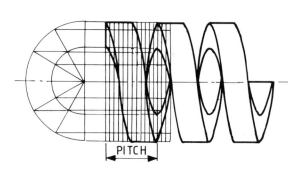

PITCH

*Right-hand square thread:*

Construct as for the right hand square spring using the same dimensions. Outline the core (centre) as shown.

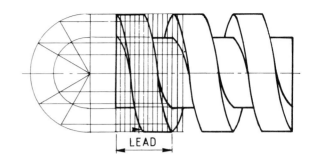

*Left-hand square spring:*

Construct using an outside diameter of 75mm and a pitch of 37mm. The thickness of the spring equals 4/12 the pitch.

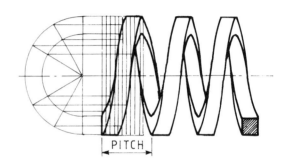

*Right hand vee thread:*

Construct a twin start vee thread given a bolt diameter of 60mm and a root diameter of 45mm.

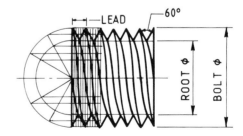

*Left hand round section spring:*

Construct given an outside diameter of 70mm and a pitch of 50mm. The cross section of the spring is 12mm diameter.

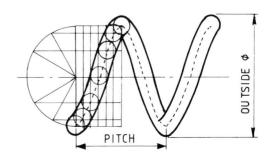

## PRACTICE 2

A helical spring is made from steel of 10mm square cross-section. The inside diameter of the coil is 60mm and the pitch is 40mm. Draw two complete turns of the spring. Hidden edges should not be shown.

*(Cambridge, November 1982)*

Ø 1m

3 m

Ø 3m

## PRACTICE 3

The spiral staircase shown in the photograph has tubular steel inner and outer handrails.

Given the following information, draw, scale 1:50, a front view of the handrails only of the staircase, with the lowest point of the staircase on the vertical centre line and to the front.

Rise of staircase during one complete turn: 3 metres
Diameter of curve of outside handrail: 3 metres
Diameter of curve of inside handrail: 1 metre
Staircase turns clockwise through 660°

*(London, June 1983)*

## PRACTICE 4

Copy each drawing on pages 54–55, using these measurements:

1. Square sides: 35mm
2. Circle diameter: 40mm
3. Distance AO: 15mm
4. Circle diameter: 50mm (Draw the normal and tangent at any convenient point.)

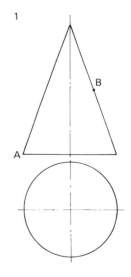

1

B

A

## PRACTICE 5

A lamp is fitted at point B on the conical church steeple shown. An electricity cable runs round the outside of the steeple from point A to the lamp.

Determine graphically and state the shortest length of cable necessary and plot its position in both plan and elevation.

*(AEB, 1981)*

## Graphical symbols

The following selection of symbols is based on British Standards Institute publication PD 7303.

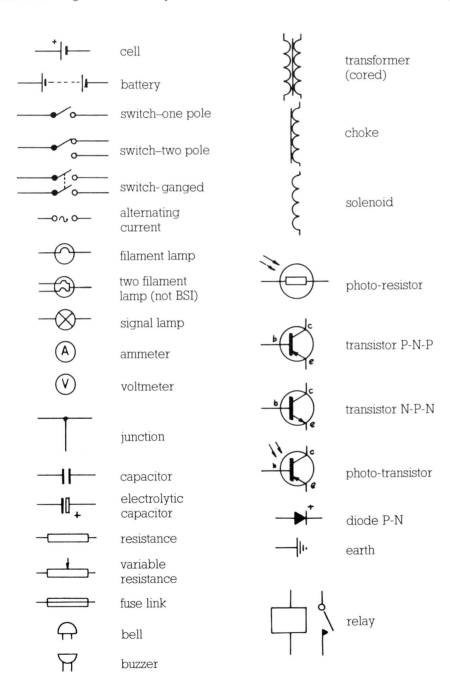

| | |
|---|---|
| cell | transformer (cored) |
| battery | choke |
| switch–one pole | solenoid |
| switch–two pole | |
| switch- ganged | |
| alternating current | photo-resistor |
| filament lamp | transistor P-N-P |
| two filament lamp (not BSI) | |
| signal lamp | transistor N-P-N |
| ammeter | |
| voltmeter | photo-transistor |
| junction | diode P-N |
| capacitor | earth |
| electrolytic capacitor | |
| resistance | relay |
| variable resistance | |
| fuse link | |
| bell | |
| buzzer | |

# Layout of circuit diagrams

Lines representing cables or conductors should be vertical or horizontal wherever possible.

Components should be positioned logically and in sequence.

Avoid conductors crossing.

The final circuit diagram should be easily read.

In the accompanying circuit diagram the cells are positioned mid-way on the vertical conductor. The switch and lamp are positioned mid-way on the horizontal conductors.

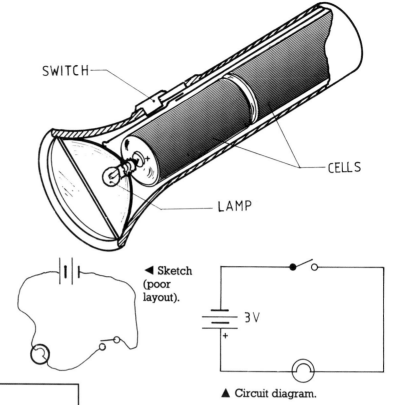

SWITCH

CELLS

LAMP

◀ Sketch (poor layout).

3V

▲ Circuit diagram.

## PRACTICE 1

The drawing shows a partly sectioned view of a torch. The lamp and the cells are connected by a switch.
Make a copy of this drawing. Sketch the torch freehand and add shading. Using instruments, draw the circuit diagram.

## PRACTICE 2

The photograph shows the various components of an electric door bell connected together.

Circuit diagram A shows the correct layout for those components.

Circuit diagram B shows the layout for a similar arrangement but with an extra bell push added for the rear door.

Connections are shown by black dots and are spaced away from other components.

Using instruments make an accurate copy of drawing B.

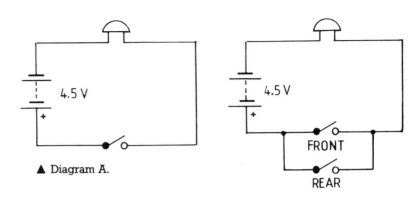

▲ Sketch  ▲ Diagram A.  ▲ Diagram B.

## PRACTICE 3

The photograph shows the various components of an electric door bell which are connected to a transformer operating from the mains.

Circuit diagram A shows the correct layout for the components.

Circuit diagram B shows the layout for a similar door bell, but with an illuminated bell push. A two-way bell push (shown as a switch) is used and it is arranged so that the lamp is normally on. When the bell push is depressed the bell is connected and the lamp is extinguished.

Make a freehand pictorial sketch of the components and wiring shown in the photograph. Using instruments, draw the circuit diagram marked B.

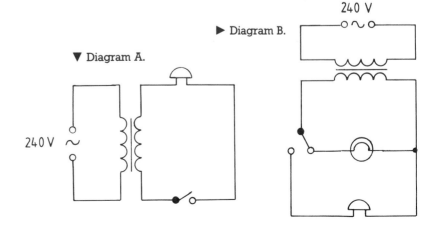

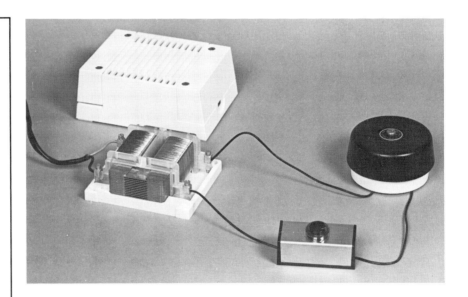

▼ Diagram A.

▶ Diagram B.

## PRACTICE 4

The photograph shows an electric filter coffee machine.

Drawing A is a sectional view taken through the machine to show the positions of the various components and the wiring. The pressure switch cuts off the supply when the water in the container above it has been used up. The mains on-off switch incorporates an indicator lamp.

Sketch B shows the position of the components using graphical symbols.

Drawing C is a circuit diagram of the arrangement with the components positioned logically and clearly.

Using instruments, draw the circuit diagram marked C.

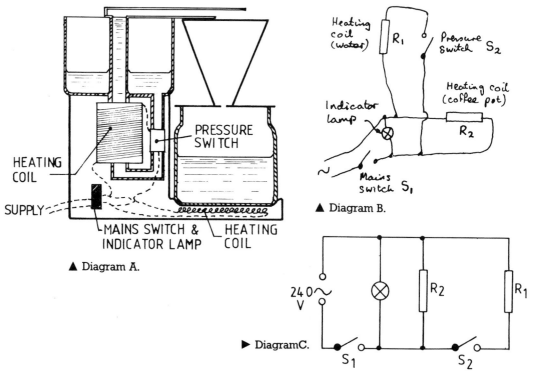

HEATING COIL

SUPPLY

PRESSURE SWITCH

MAINS SWITCH & INDICATOR LAMP

HEATING COIL

▲ Diagram A.

Heating coil (water) R₁

Pressure switch S₂

Heating coil (coffee pot) R₂

Indicator lamp

~ Mains switch S₁

▲ Diagram B.

240~V ⊗ R₂ R₁ S₁ S₂

▶ Diagram C.

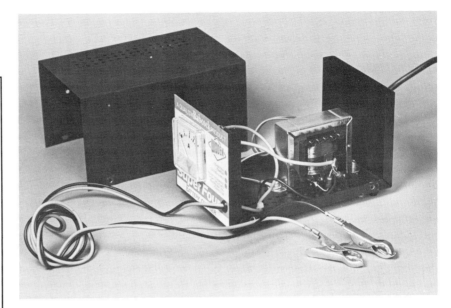

## PRACTICE 5

The photograph shows a simple battery charger with the cover removed to show the components and the wiring.

A circuit diagram of the arrangement has been drawn starting with the mains supply and finishing with the outlet terminals of the battery charger.

The polarity of the diode is shown and this will determine the polarity of the outlet terminals. A fuse is used to protect the diode against overload or short circuit.

Make a freehand pictorial sketch of the body of the battery charger with the cover replaced. Using instruments, draw the circuit diagram for the battery charger, showing a 12 volt battery connected to the output terminals.

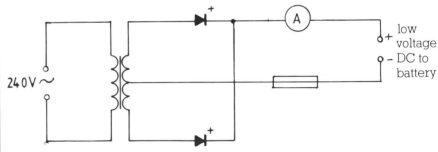

240V ~

low voltage DC to battery

# Motor vehicle circuits

## Parking lamps

On the outline plan, the positions of the front and rear lamps, battery, fuse and switch are shown. The body of the vehicle is used as the return connection to the battery. This is usually referred to as the earth.

A circuit diagram of the arrangement is shown on the right.

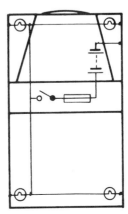

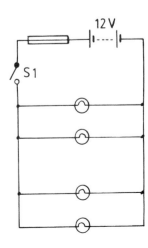

## Headlamps

The headlamps consist of lamps with two filaments. One filament for the dip position and the other for the full beam position. A two-way switch S3 allows the lamps to be switched to either position. Switch S2 is the on-off switch.

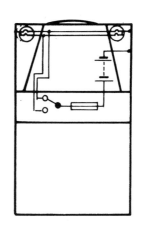
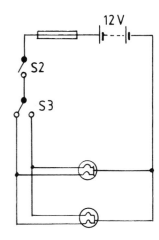

## Direction indicator

The flasher unit marked F can be treated as a black box and its circuitry can be ignored. Its function is to cause the lights to flash on and off at regular intervals. Switch S4 is a three position switch with the centre position off. It is also a two pole switch, one pole controls the lights and the other pole controls the flasher unit.

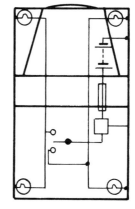
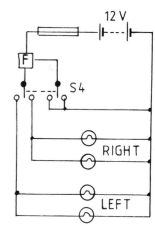

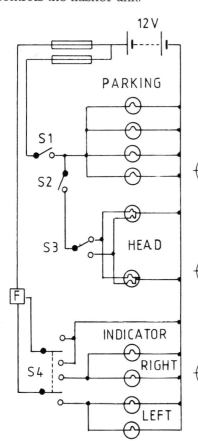

▲ Combination of all circuits.

### PRACTICE 1

Draw the circuit diagram for the headlamps.
Draw the circuit diagram for the direction indicator.

### PRACTICE 2

Draw the combined circuit on the left for parking lights, headlamps and direction indicator.

### PRACTICE 3

In a similar manner to practice 1 and 2 design and draw circuits for: horn, wipers (front and rear), rear fog lights. The wipers and horn will be on the same fuse and the fog lights will be on a separate fuse. Invent your own symbols for horn and wipers.

## House wiring

The photograph shows, from left to right some of the common electrical fittings used in house wiring.

Light switch, 13 amp socket, consumer unit, ceiling rose and light fitting.

### Lighting circuit

Circuit diagram A shows the switching arrangement for room lighting. Switches S1, S2, S3 each control single lamps, one for each room. Switch S4 controls two lamps, this could be a living room.

Note:

The fuse and the switches are always on the live (L) side of the circuit and the wiring is coloured red. The wiring from the switch to the lampholder is also coloured red. The return cable from the lampholder which is called the neutral (N), is always coloured black. Colour conventions for flexible cables are live = brown, neutral = blue and earth = green and yellow.

### Two-way switching

Circuit diagram B is a two-way switching circuit for use on stairways. Movement of either switch will control the lighting on or off.

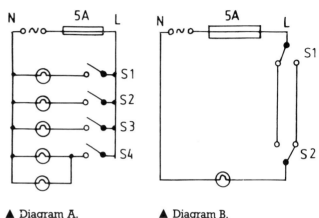

▲ Diagram A.     ▲ Diagram B.

PRACTICE 1

Make an accurate drawing of the two circuit diagrams A and B.

### Ring circuit

As shown in the drawing here, the ring circuit starts at the fuse box and the cables are looped from one socket outlet to the next, finishing at the fuse box. Both ends of the cable are connected to the same fuse, rating 30 amps.

A twin socket is considered as single unit for planning purposes.

Institute of Electrical Engineers regulations govern the number of socket outlets on a ring main. The predicted loading of the circuit will be one of the main factors.

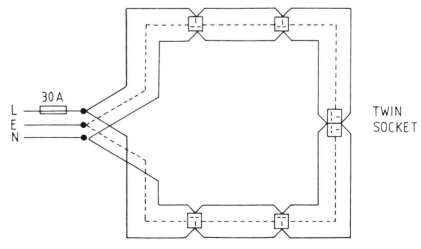

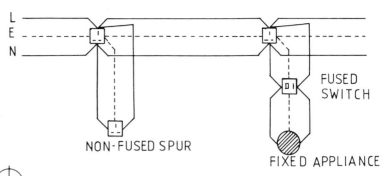

NON-FUSED SPUR

FUSED SWITCH

FIXED APPLIANCE

## Spurs

Additional socket outlets can be taken from socket outlets in the ring main. This arrangement is referred to as a spur.

When a fixed appliance eg. ventilator fan, is connected to the ring main as a spur, a fused isolator switch is necessary. The rating of the fuse will depend upon the appliance.

**PRACTICE 2**

Make an accurate drawing of the ring circuit. Use colours for the wiring: red for live, black for neutral and yellow and green (dotted) for the earth.

## Circuit diagram for a small dwelling unit

This drawing shows a typical circuit diagram of the wiring for a small house or flat.

All circuits start from the consumer unit which consists of fuses and terminal connections for the cables. The unit is connected to the mains supply by means of a two pole switch.

The ring circuit starts and terminates at the same terminals in the consumer unit. The fuse rating would normally be 30 amps. The ring circuit supplies all the socket outlets in the house. Two spurs have been taken: one for two single sockets and the other for a fan through a fused switch.

Two separate lighting circuits are shown. One would be for the ground floor and the other for the first floor of the house. Each circuit would be protected by a fuse rating 5 amps.

The cooker is supplied by a separate circuit and an isolating switch. The rating of the fuse would be 30 amps.

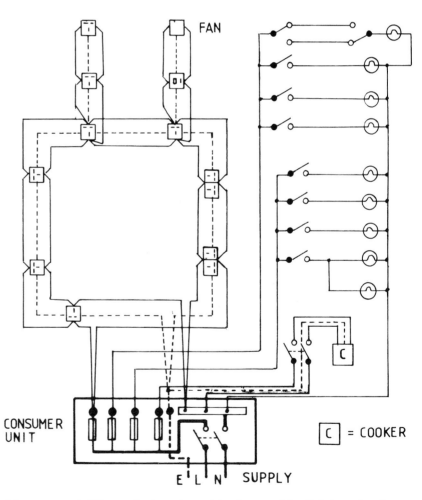

FAN

CONSUMER UNIT

E  L  N   SUPPLY

[C] = COOKER

*Note:* an earth (E) supply (not shown) is also used for lighting circuits.

 PRACTICE 3

Make a circuit diagram of the electrical wiring in your home. The diagram should be based on the drawing shown on page 66.

If you live in a house select the ground floor. If you live in a bungalow, or flat select the kitchen and three other rooms.

You will need to use your own judgement as to the layout of the ring circuit and the fusing arrangements.

*Do NOT tamper with the electrical fittings at home.*

## Kitchen plan (1)

This drawing is an architect's plan of the kitchen shown on the next page.

Note that the electrical installation symbols shown here are different from the circuit symbols used elsewhere in this chapter and the cable runs have been shown as single lines.

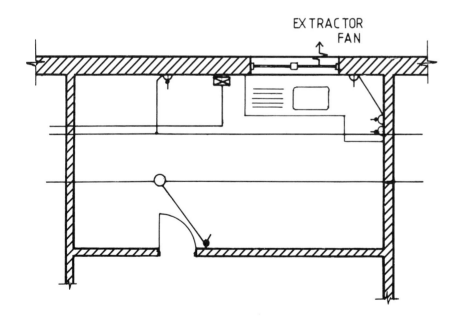

 PRACTICE 4

To a suitable scale make a freehand sketch of the plan of your kitchen at home. Using the correct symbols, (see page 33), mark the electrical fittings in their correct positions. Indicate cable runs – this may not be obvious and you should use your own judgement.

## Kitchen plan (2)

The planometric drawing of a kitchen (p. 67) shows the positions of the various electrical fittings and the wiring.

The ring circuit is fed from the consumer unit to two socket outlets and a fused spur. It then continues to the other rooms of the house and finally returns to the consumer unit.

The cooker supply is fed directly from the consumer unit to an isolating cooker switch.

The lighting circuit is fed from the consumer unit to the first ceiling rose where a connection is made to the on-off switch. The supply then continues to the other rooms of the house. More than one lighting circuit may be necessary, depending on the number of rooms and the total estimated loading in the house.

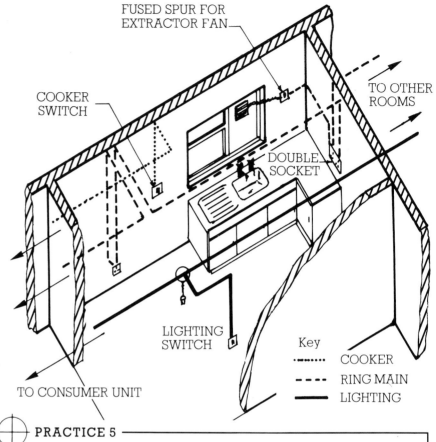

FUSED SPUR FOR
EXTRACTOR FAN

COOKER
SWITCH

TO OTHER
ROOMS

DOUBLE
SOCKET

LIGHTING
SWITCH

TO CONSUMER UNIT

Key

......... COOKER
- - - - RING MAIN
LIGHTING

### PRACTICE 5

From the sketch in the previous question make an accurate planometric drawing of your kitchen and mark in the electrical fittings and cable runs.

# Electronic circuits

## Simple amplifier

The photograph and sketch show the components of a simple amplifier connected together.

A circuit diagram of the arrangement is shown on the next page.

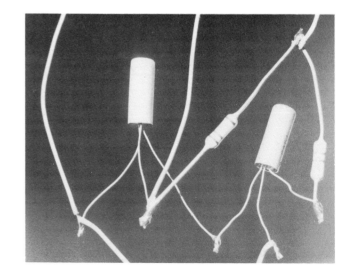

Components should be labelled, the polarity of the circuit should be indicated and the layout should be clear and logical.

Note: Connections (eg. between R2 and TR2) should be made away from transistors.

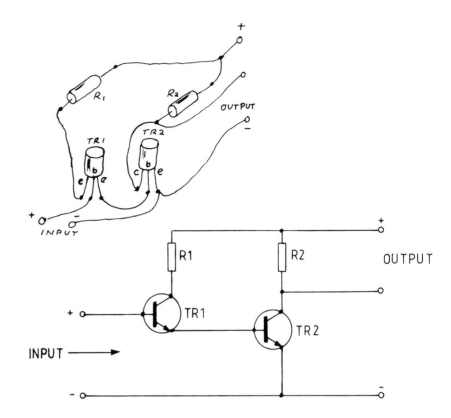

 **PRACTICE 1**

Using instruments, make a copy of the circuit diagram.

## Multivibrator

The photograph and sketch show the various components of a multivibrator or oscillator.

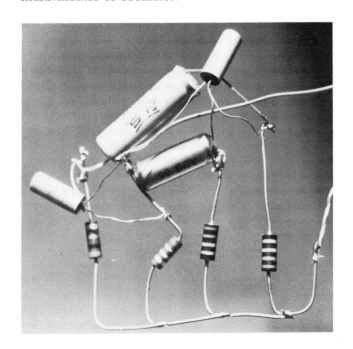

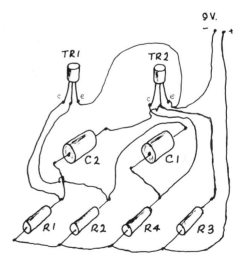

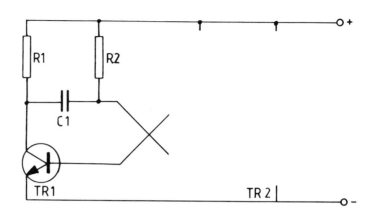

PRACTICE 2

The circuit diagram has been partly drawn. Make a drawing showing the complete circuit.

▲ Circuit board and components.

▲ Reverse side of board showing printed circuit.

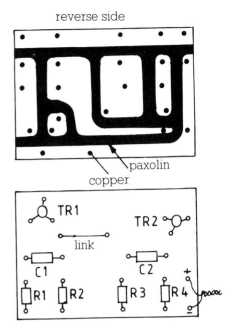

reverse side

paxolin

copper

## Circuit boards

It is normal to mount the various components on a board and not to have them in the jumbled mess as shown in the previous example. The photographs on the previous page show an example of a circuit board. If there is a fault with the circuit, the board is simply removed from the equipment and is usually replaced with a new one.

The drawings show three different circuit boards of the components for the multivibrator on the previous pages.

In this example one side of the paxolin board of thickness 1 – 2mm is coated with a thin layer of copper. The copper is etched away to leave the 'wiring'. Holes are drilled for components which are soldered to the copper.

In this example the amount of copper conductor has been kept to a minimum. This has the advantage of allowing the circuit to be traced more easily.

conductor

reverse side

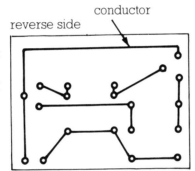

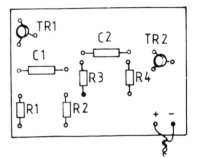

Stripboard is used here. Parallel strips of copper are attached to an insulating board (paxolin). Holes are drilled for components and the strips can be cut to provide additional circuitry.

paxolin    copper

reverse side

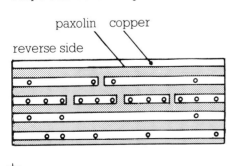

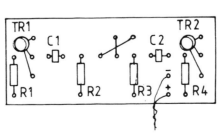

## PRACTICE 3

For the amplifier on page 57, design and draw circuit boards. Three drawings should be produced, one for each type of board shown.

# Circuits for different purposes

 PRACTICE 1 ————————————

The drawing shows the outline of a bicycle with a dynamo, headlamp and rear lamp. The dynamo is of the friction drive type and it is disengaged from the wheel when the lights are to be off. The frame of the cycle is used as one of the conductors.

Make a circuit diagram of the lighting arrangement. The symbol shown should be used for the dynamo.

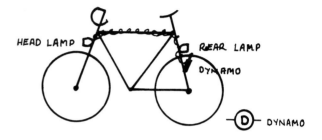

HEAD LAMP    REAR LAMP    DYNAMO

—(D)— DYNAMO

PRACTICE 2 ————————————

The sketch shows a cue lighting system for use in a small theatre, between the stage manager and the lighting operator. The arrangement consists of a push switch, which can be shown by the conventional sign for a switch, and a 12 volt lamp connected to a transformer which is plugged into the mains.

Draw a circuit diagram of the system, including the transformer and switch.

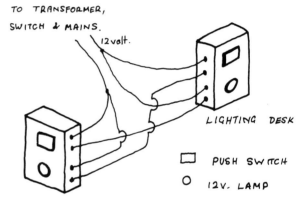

TO TRANSFORMER, SWITCH & MAINS.

12 volt.

LIGHTING DESK

STAGE MANAGER.

☐ PUSH SWITCH

○ 12V. LAMP

PRACTICE 3 ————————————

The sketch shows the various components for an electric iron. Make a circuit diagram of the arrangement starting from the 240 volt mains supply.

The heating coil should be shown as a resistance and the thermostat should be shown as a switch in the closed position and labelled 'thermostat'.

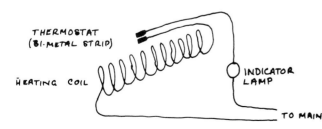

THERMOSTAT (BI-METAL STRIP)

HEATING COIL

INDICATOR LAMP

TO MAINS.

PRACTICE 4

A sketch showing the electrical circuit of an
overhead projector is given. The fan is earthed to
the supply through the case of the projector.

Select from the electrical symbols given to draw a
wiring diagram of the circuit.

*(London, June 1982)*

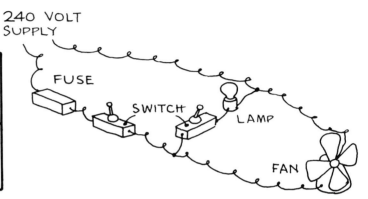

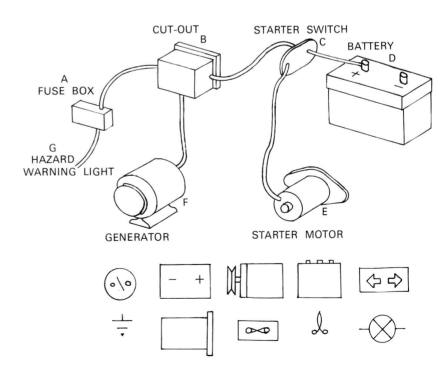

 PRACTICE 5

The diagram shows part of a
car's electrical system. The car
body is used as an earth return.

The battery, generator, starter
motor and hazard light are all
earthed to the car body. These
connections are not shown.

Construct a schematic wiring
diagram of the system shown.
Select and enter the most
appropriate symbol to
represent the items of
equipment.

Show the necessary
connections to the body in your
drawing.

*(AEB, 1981)*

# 6 ⊕ Vectors

## Vector diagrams

> A *scalar* quantity is one which has magnitude only.
> For example a temperature of 23° C.
> A *vector* quantity has magnitude and direction.
> For example, a wind of 30km/hr blowing from the north.

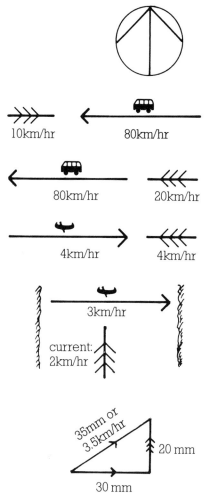

North should be assumed to be as indicated on the diagram.

1. A bus is travelling due west along the M4 at 80km/hr against a headwind from the west of 10km/hr. Its actual speed will be 70km/hr assuming no additional engine power is used.

2. The same bus travelling west at 80km/hr is now subjected to a tail wind of 20km/hr from the east. Its actual speed is 100km/hr.

3. The maximum speed a boy can paddle the canoe in calm water is 4km/hr. The boy now attempts to paddle the canoe up the River Severn which is flowing at 4km/hr. The canoe will remain stationary.

4. The maximum speed of the canoe in calm water is 3km/hr. A boy attempts to cross the River Trent from bank to bank. The river is flowing at a speed of 2km/hr.
   The following will happen to the canoe:
   (a) It will be driven off course by the current.
   (b) It will move faster.

   To determine these two factors a vector diagram can be drawn. The direction and magnitude of the canoe and the current can be represented on a scale drawing as shown. The third side of the triangle indicates the direction and speed of the canoe.

   A suitable scale is chosen for this drawing. In this case 10mm represents 1km/hr.

5. An aeroplane on a course from west to east is subject to a wind from the south-west. To determine the actual course and speed of the aircraft a scale drawing is produced as shown below. The direction and speed of the aircraft are drawn to a scale of 1mm represents 5km/hr.

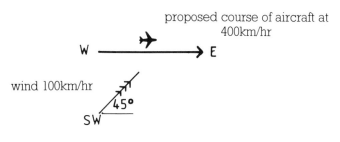

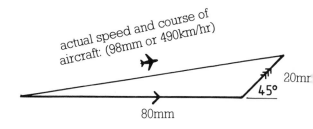

6. The same aircraft flying on a course from west to east is now subject to a wind from the north-east. Its speed will be reduced and it will be blown off course. The actual speed and direction of the aircraft can be determined by the scale drawing shown below.

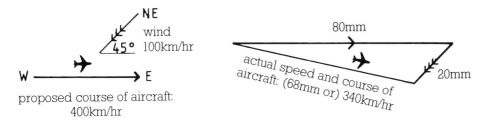

7. This example is the basis of navigation problem-solving. The required route of the aircraft is from west to east at a speed of 400km/hr, it is subject to a wind of 100km/hr from the north-east. Determine the speed and course necessary for the aircraft to arrive at its correct destination.

   The vectors are drawn to scale as shown and the closing link of the triangle will give the direction and speed (drawn to scale) of the aircraft.

   Similar problems can be solved to determine distance travelled.

   Note: For the purpose of simplicity, values for wind speed, currents and aircraft speed have been given in km/hr. In practice, knots and other specialist measurements are used.

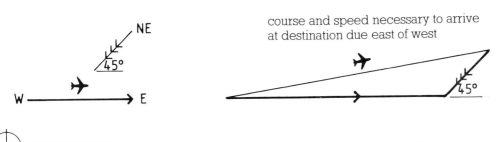

⊕ **PRACTICE 1**

Draw examples 5, 6 and 7 using the information given.

⊕ **PRACTICE 2**

Determine the actual speed and direction of a boat heading from north to south at a speed of 6km/hr and subject to a wind of 3km/hr from the south-west. How far will it have travelled after 3 hours?

# Force diagrams

The drawing shows two forces of 3 newtons and 5 newtons angled at 60° to each other and acting on a point P.

## The resultant

To determine the resultant, or a single force that would replace the two forces in magnitude and direction, a parallelogram is drawn. A scale drawing of the forces is made and the diagonal of the parallogram represents the resultant in magnitude and direction.

In this case 10mm represents 1 newton.

Resultant: 70mm or 7 newtons.

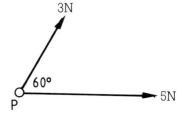

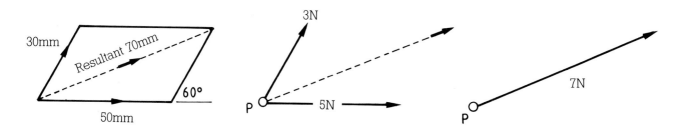

The resultant is shown as a dotted line. It could replace the two forces.

## Equilibrium

For point P to be in a state of equilibrium (it cannot move) an opposite force must exist. This is shown by the direction and magnitude of the resultant at point P.

P will be in a state of equilibrium when equal and opposite forces act on it.

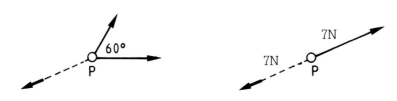

Resultant 7N

## Worked examples

1. In the drawing below two forces A and B are separated by an angle of 105° and are acting on a point P. The force necessary to keep the system in equilibrium is shown by the dotted line or resultant.

A = 60 newtons
B = 40 newtons
Resultant: 30mm or 60 newtons
Scale: 20 newtons = 10mm

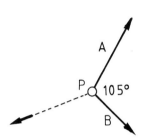
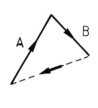

An alternative and more convenient method of finding the resultant is to draw a triangle to scale.

The lengths of lines A and B indicate the forces in newtons. Their position shows the direction of the forces.
For a point to be in a state of equilibrium the arrows on the force and resultant lines must follow each other.

Procedure: From the estimated position of the resultant and in a clockwise direction, mark the forces A and B. Draw them in the order starting at A. The line (dotted) closing the triangle will be the resultant and its magnitude and direction can be read off.

2. In the drawing below the two forces A and B are replaced by a single or resultant force shown by the dotted line.

A = 60 newtons
B = 40 newtons
APB = 105°

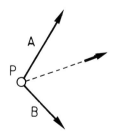
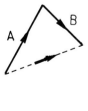

The procedure is the same as the previous drawing except the direction of the arrow for the resultant (dotted) is opposite.

3. The drawing below shows three forces A, B and C acting at a point. The force necessary to keep the system in equilibrium is called the resultant and is shown by the dotted line.

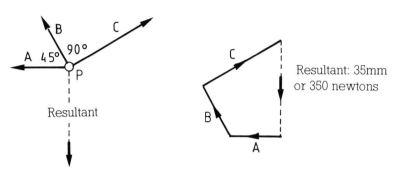

| | FORCE newtons | SCALE 1mm = 10N |
|---|---|---|
| A | 200N | 20mm |
| B | 200N | 20mm |
| C | 350N | 35mm |

Resultant: 35mm or 350 newtons

To determine the value and the direction of the resultant a polygon is drawn to scale. The procedure and rules are the same as for triangle of force diagrams.

4. The four forces A, B, C and D are kept in equilibrium by the resultant R. The value of R is found by drawing to a suitable scale a polygon starting at A. The closing link of the polygon will give the direction and magnitude of the resultant.

A = 6 newtons
B = 2 newtons
C = 6 newtons
D = 5 newtons

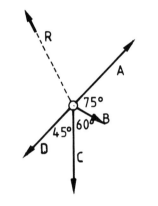
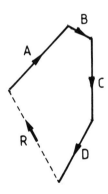

5. In this case the forces A, B and C acting at a point are kept at equilibrium by the two forces D and E at right angles to each other. To determine the values of D and E the polygon is drawn in the usual way with forces D and E being the closing links.

A = 40 newtons
B = 60 newtons
C = 80 newtons

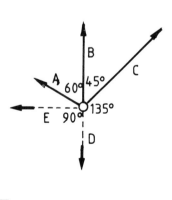
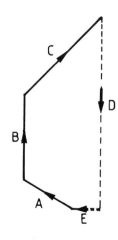

⊕ PRACTICE ─────────

Draw out each of the examples shown using the values given.

# 7 Flow charts

## Using data processing symbols

The flow charts in this chapter refer to processes of a practical nature. Data processing symbols have been used for the various operations.

The following rules apply to flow charts:
1. The layout should be as clear as possible.
2. Proportions for the symbols should be consistent.
3. Avoid lines crossing.
4. Arrows indicate the direction of flow.
5. A vertical chart starts at the top.
6. A horizontal chart starts on the left hand side.

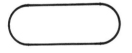

▲ Terminal: This symbol indicates the beginning and end in a process.

▲ Process: this symbol represents general processes without specifying method or equipment.

The example shows the use of terminal and process symbols in a vertical chart.

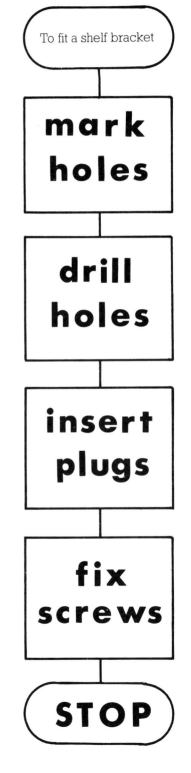

To fit a shelf bracket

mark holes

drill holes

insert plugs

fix screws

STOP

This example shows the layout for the Green Cross Code chart.

The decision symbol is used and there is always a 'Yes' or 'No' response.

Feedback has been used to return the process to an earlier part of the chart. Arrows show the direction of flow.

◀ **Decision: this symbol represents a decision or switching type operation.**

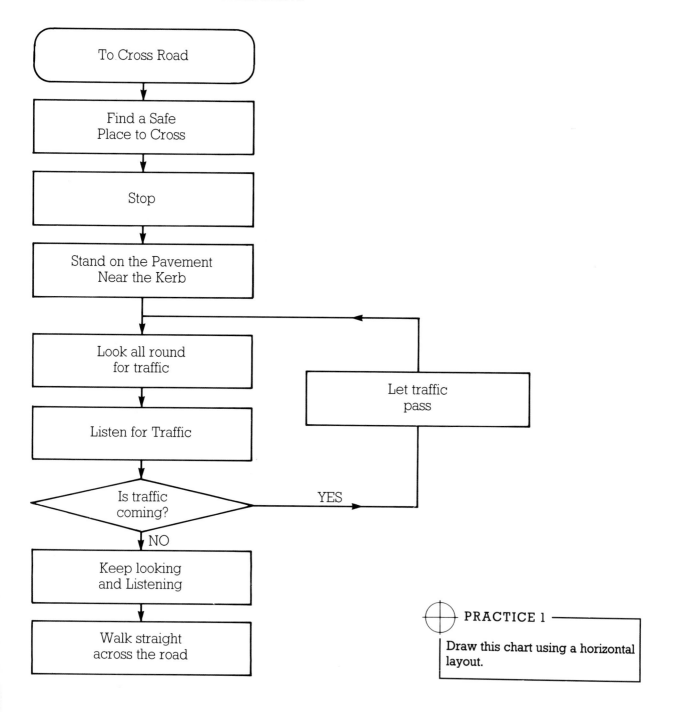

PRACTICE 1

Draw this chart using a horizontal layout.

This example shows the use of connectors to enable a long chart to fit into a convenient space. The connectors are labelled. The input/output symbol is also shown.

◀ Connector: this symbol represents the entry or exit from another part of a flow chart.

◀ Input/output: this symbol is used to represent any kind of input or output.

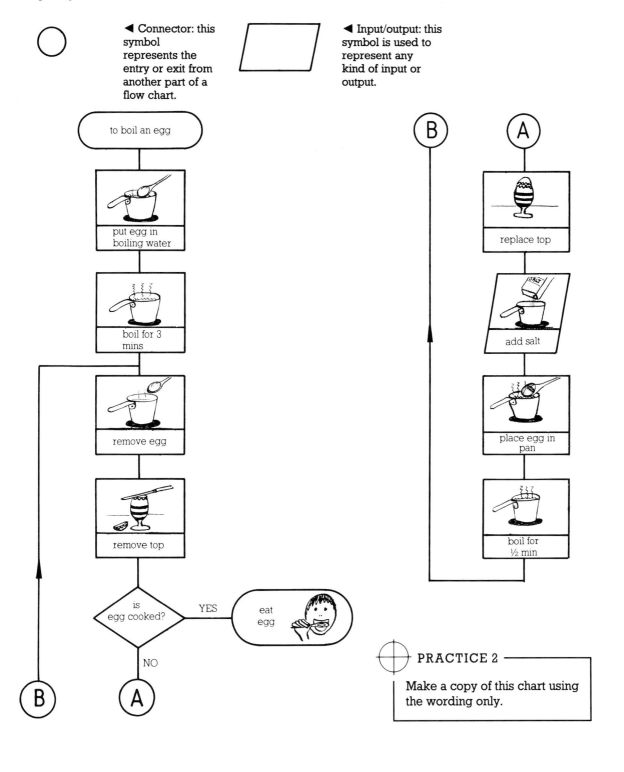

to boil an egg

put egg in boiling water

boil for 3 mins

remove egg

remove top

is egg cooked?   YES   eat egg

NO

B        A

B        A

replace top

add salt

place egg in pan

boil for ½ min

PRACTICE 2

Make a copy of this chart using the wording only.

This example shows another method of layout when using connectors.

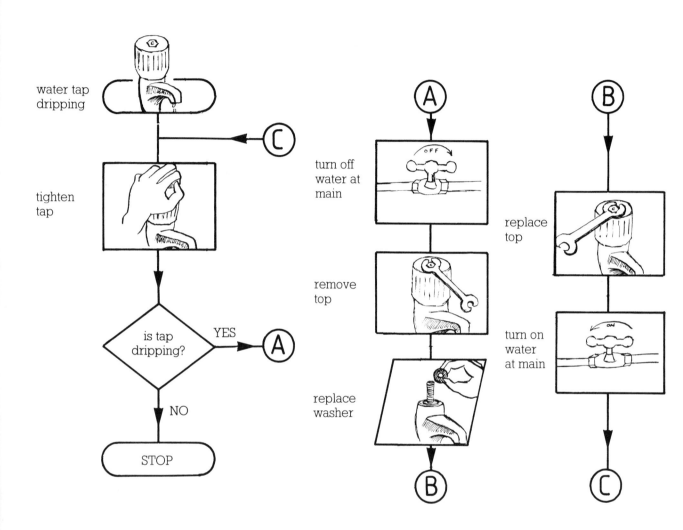

⊕ PRACTICE 3

Draw the chart including the working, but without using connectors or illustrations.

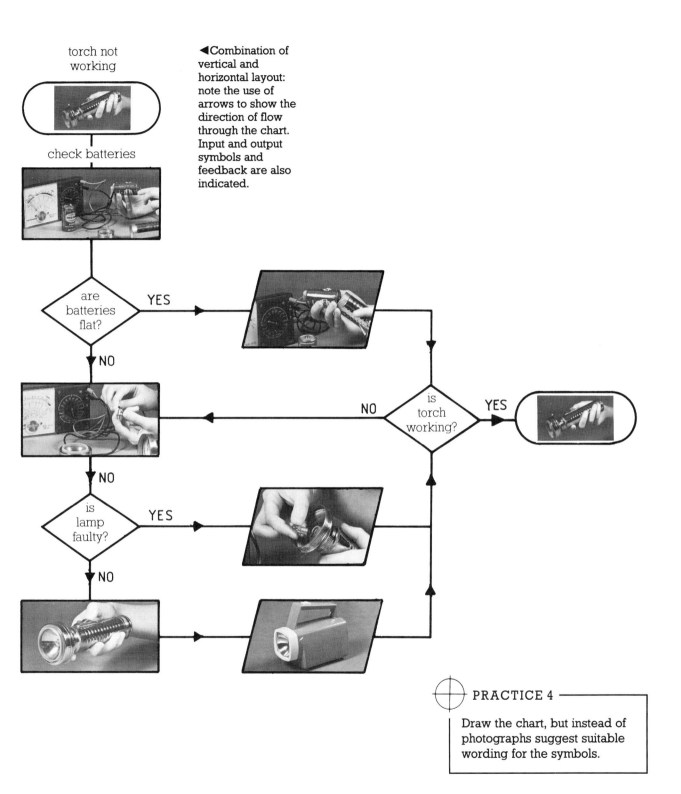

torch not working

check batteries

◄Combination of vertical and horizontal layout: note the use of arrows to show the direction of flow through the chart. Input and output symbols and feedback are also indicated.

are batteries flat? — YES

NO

is torch working? — YES

NO

is lamp faulty? — YES

NO

The chart below is based on critical path analysis. A, B, C travel by different means to the same bus stop, they travel by bus, A and C walk to school, B takes a different route. D cycles directly to school.

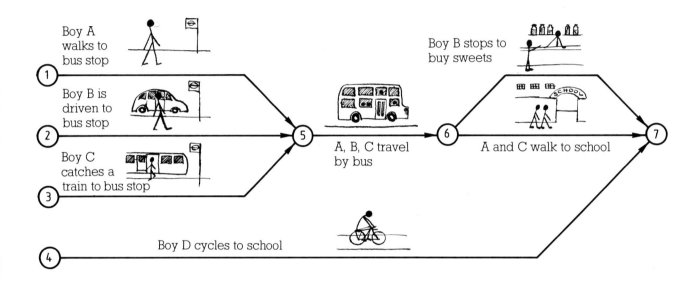

## Gannt chart

The chart on the right is called a Gantt chart. In this example the chart shows the comparative travelling times by four boys to school. The shaded area indicates boys A, B, C, travel on the same bus for the same length of time. The starting and arrival times for each boy is different.

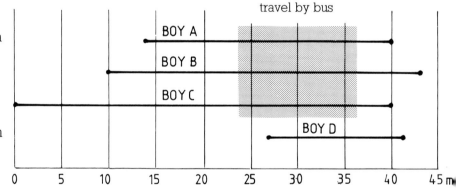

⊕ PRACTICE 5 ─────────────────────────

Draw similar charts to those shown above. Include four or more pupils in your class, use illustrations and colour.

## Organisation charts

The chart below is an example of part of an organisation chart for the Scout movement.

### PRACTICE 6

1. Draw the part of the chart which is shown as a heavy outline.
2. Draw an organisation chart to show the lines of responsibility at your school. Start with the headteacher.

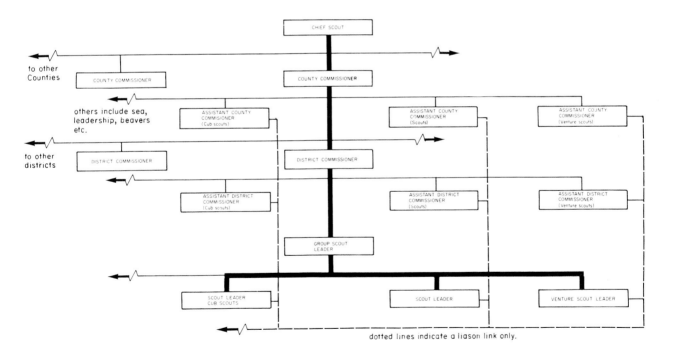

## Production chart

The production chart shows the various steps for making a salt pot in the school workshop.

The salt pot consists of three separate parts –
Part A the body.
Part B the nut.
Part C the screw.
The various steps for making each part are shown in the chart. When all the parts have been made the salt pot is assembled.

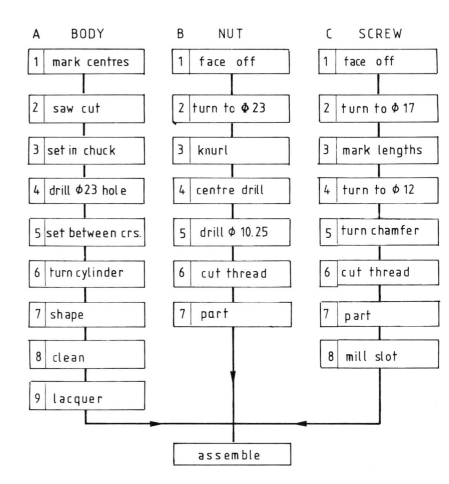

| A | BODY |
|---|---|
| 1 | mark centres |
| 2 | saw cut |
| 3 | set in chuck |
| 4 | drill φ23 hole |
| 5 | set between crs. |
| 6 | turn cylinder |
| 7 | shape |
| 8 | clean |
| 9 | lacquer |

| B | NUT |
|---|---|
| 1 | face off |
| 2 | turn to φ 23 |
| 3 | knurl |
| 4 | centre drill |
| 5 | drill φ 10.25 |
| 6 | cut thread |
| 7 | part |

| C | SCREW |
|---|---|
| 1 | face off |
| 2 | turn to φ 17 |
| 3 | mark lengths |
| 4 | turn to φ 12 |
| 5 | turn chamfer |
| 6 | cut thread |
| 7 | part |
| 8 | mill slot |

assemble

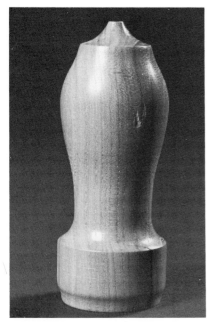

A BODY

B NUT

C SCREW

The critical path analysis chart shows each part being made at the same time by separate operators. If one person were to make the salt pot, the numbers would follow each other.

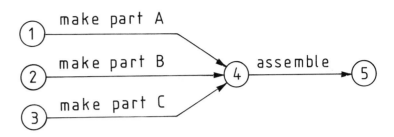

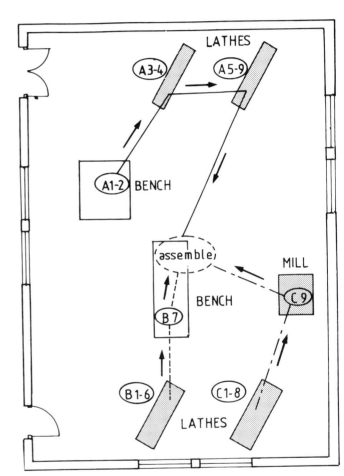

The simplified plan of a workshop shows the movement of the various parts in the workshop during manufacture.
The various operations have been letter coded according to the production chart.

## PRACTICE 7

For the item of craftwork you are making at the moment, list all the processes involved and present them in the form of a production chart.

Make a scale drawing of the school workshop, indicate the principal machines and draw a flow diagram to show movement in the workshop to produce the item of craftwork.
Colour and shading can be used.

## Fluid systems

Various symbols are used for the components in fluid charts and they have been labelled on the drawings where appropriate.

Wherever possible, lines should not cross. The components should be laid out logically and clearly.

The sketch shows the various components for a domestic heating system. In this simplified drawing, only four radiators are shown.

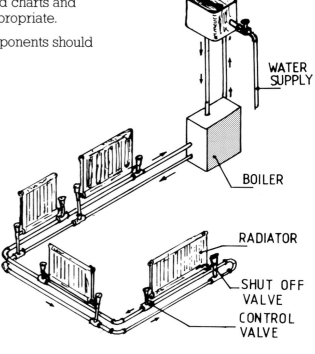

This is a graphical diagram of the arrangement. Symbols have been used for the valves and radiators.

*Note:* The control valves have been omitted in this diagram.

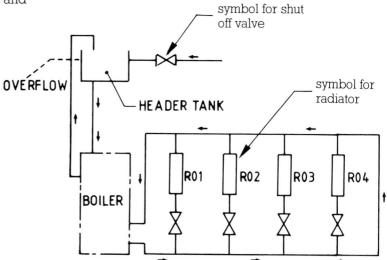

Symbols have been used on this three dimensional drawing of the arrangement.

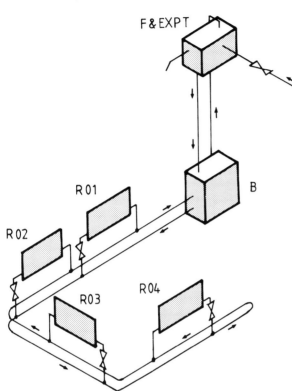

PRACTICE 8

Make a three dimensional sketch of the cold water system in your home. Include the cold tank, wash basin, sink, bath and WC.

Show the system as a diagram using graphical symbols.

A plan of a building showing the positions of the radiators, boiler and expansion tank. Building drawing symbols have been used and pipe runs have not been shown.

PRACTICE 9

To a convenient scale make a freehand sketch of the plan and show the various components for the central heating including the pipe runs.

MEETING HALL

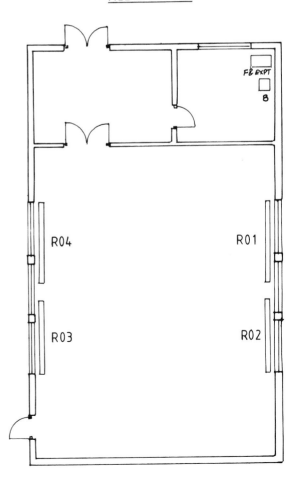

The drawing below shows the gas/air system for a brazing hearth used in a school workshop. Graphical symbols have been used and the diagram reads from left to right.

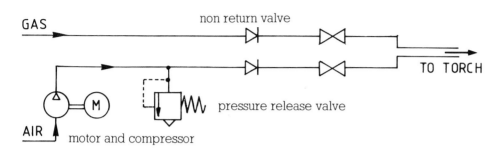

---

⊕ PRACTICE 10 ——————————————————————

Using instruments make a copy of the drawing shown above. Use technical pens.

---

⊕ PRACTICE 11 ——————————————————————

The following sequence of events occur when a married couple get up in the morning. They have only one wash basin available.

Husband and wife get up together. The wife puts the kettle on, makes the tea, washes before her husband, gets dressed, cooks the breakfast, eats breakfast and washes up. The husband washes, shaves, gets dressed, eats breakfast, prepares to leave and leaves for the office.

The tea is made and whilst it brews the wife washes, gets dressed and cooks. Both sit down to breakfast at the same time.

Each activity takes one unit of time except cooking, eating breakfast and washing up which each take two units of time.

(a) Draw a FLOW DIAGRAM, using letters from the list below to represent activities, of the sequence of events detailed above.

(A) put kettle on; (B) make tea; (C) cook breakfast; (D) wash up; (E) husband gets up; (F) husband eats breakfast; (G) wife gets up; (H) wife gets dressed; (I) wife washes; (J) wife eats breakfast; (K) husband shaves; (L) husband leaves for office; (M) husband prepares to leave; (N) tea brews; (O) husband washes; (P) husband gets dressed.

(b) State the minimum number of units of time needed by the couple to complete the sequence.

*(AEB, June 1982)*

---

⊕ PRACTICE 12 ——————

Make a study of your parents' movements in the kitchen while preparing the evening meal. Draw a plan scale 1:50 of your kitchen and show the various kitchen fittings. By means of arrows, indicate the movement around the kitchen. Can the kitchen be redesigned to cut the amount of movement down to a minimum?

## PRACTICE 13

Notes from a leaflet for children on dental care procedures are given, out of sequence, below:

Brush well, particularly in the vertical direction.

Place a bristle length of good quality toothpaste on the brush.

Go to the privacy of your bathroom.

The next procedure is to rinse the mouth properly.

If your teeth are clean you may leave the bathroom.

If your teeth are not clean you should repeat the procedure as necessary. You may then leave the bathroom.

You should always check, use the mirror, this will help you decide whether or not your teeth are clean.

Arrange the above rather wordy procedures in a logical sequence. Show the sequence in the form of a simple flow diagram.

Use the base symbols given. Arrows are only required if the flow lines are not drawn in the usually accepted direction.

Each symbol should have only one or two words printed inside. Odd words may be placed on the flow lines if thought necessary.

*(AEB, June 1982)*

DECISION

START & STOP

PROCEDURE

## PRACTICE 14

The drawing shows some of the water pipes used in a domestic water system. Solid lines represent the pipes. Cold water is supplied from the mains via stop cock to a storage tank A, from there to a cylinder B and thence to the bottom of a boiler C. The water is then heated and rises via the pipe at the top of the boiler C to the cylinder B. Hot water can then be drawn off for the taps at the wash basin D, sink unit E, and the bath F. Cold water is supplied to the sink unit E by a branch pipe from the main supply pipe. The toilet, G, wash basin, D, and bath, F, are supplied from the tank A.

In the event of the water overheating it will continue to rise and be discharged into tank A.

Construct a circuit diagram of the system. Select and letter the most appropriate symbols from these given below and indicate by arrows the direction of the flow, and by colour which pipes are part of the hot water system and which are part of the cold water system.

Show the pipes leading to the taps but do not show the taps.

*(AEB, 1982)*

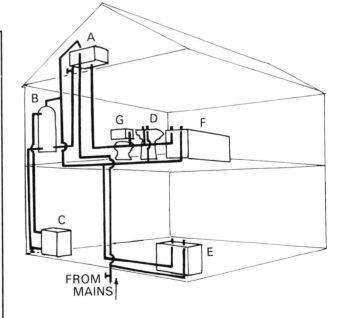

## Illustrations relating to processes

The illustration shows a series of instructions for using a coffee filter machine.

   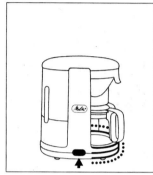

▲ How to use your coffee machine.

▲ Remove water tank and fill to the required level.

▲ Place filter paper in container and add the required amount of filter fine coffee.

▲ Switch on.

 PRACTICE 1

A publisher is considering the possibility of marketing a cookery book for people who have difficulty in understanding written instructions. It is proposed that any sequence to be conveyed is set out as a series of drawings without any words and arranged so that the stages can be followed clearly without confusion.

The sequence for making a single mug of tea, according to the method set out in List C below, is to be prepared for market research purposes.

The first stage in the sequence is shown below to indicate the size of each drawing and the style to adopt.

Complete the sequence, deciding for yourself the number of stages to be drawn and bearing in mind that numerals and colour may be used if desired.

List C:

Fill the kettle; heat the kettle; fetch a mug, a spoon, a teabag, the sugar and the milk; put the teabag in the mug; when the water boils, add it to mug; allow to stand for three minutes; remove the teabag; add sugar; add milk; stir.

*(Cambridge, 1982)*

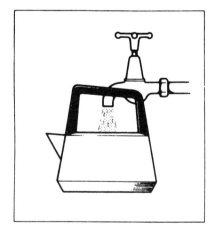

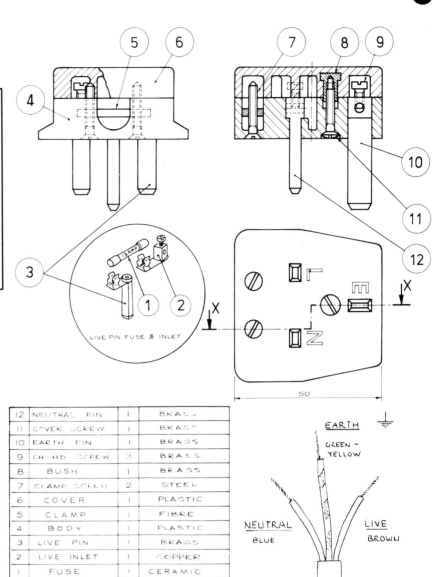

## PRACTICE 2

Maintenance manuals and DIY books often contain sketches to show how a process is logically followed through. Study the orthographic drawings of a 13 amp plug and produce a series of sketches to illustrate the process of wiring an appliance to the amp plug. The appliance has a three core cable.

*(North Regional Exam Board, 1983)*

LIVE PIN, FUSE & INLET

| REF | ITEM | QTY | MATERIAL |
|---|---|---|---|
| 12 | NEUTRAL PIN | 1 | BRASS |
| 11 | COVER SCREW | 1 | BRASS |
| 10 | EARTH PIN | 1 | BRASS |
| 9 | CH HD SCREW | 3 | BRASS |
| 8 | BUSH | 1 | BRASS |
| 7 | CLAMP SCREW | 2 | STEEL |
| 6 | COVER | 1 | PLASTIC |
| 5 | CLAMP | 1 | FIBRE |
| 4 | BODY | 1 | PLASTIC |
| 3 | LIVE PIN | 1 | BRASS |
| 2 | LIVE INLET | 1 | COPPER |
| 1 | FUSE | 1 | CERAMIC |

EARTH
GREEN – YELLOW

NEUTRAL
BLUE

LIVE
BROWN

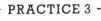

## PRACTICE 3

The photograph shows a corner joint for joining chipboard.

By means of freehand sketches and simple notes (no more than three words) produce a series of illustrations for an instruction leaflet to show how the joint can be fixed.

# 8 ⊕ True length of lines

## First angle projection

The drawing shows the plan and elevation of a line AB projected into the vertical plane (VP) and the horizontal plane (HP).

AB is a line on an inclined plane. The projections of the line in the vertical plane and the horizontal plane are shown.

AB is a line which is inclined to both the horizontal and vertical planes.

The traces of line AB produced by the two inclined planes is shown.

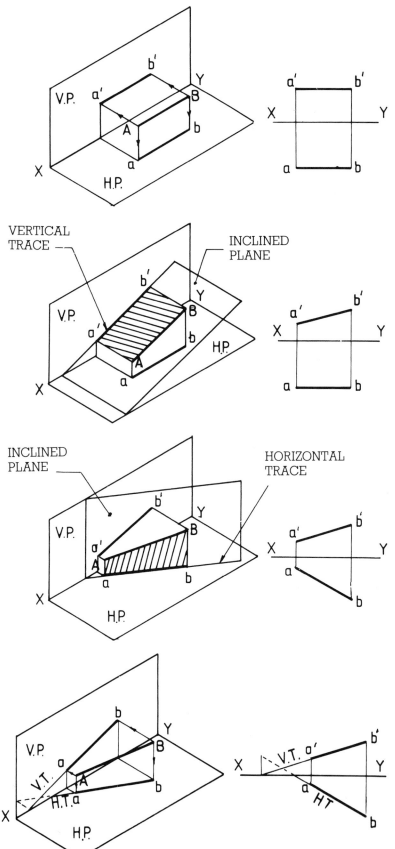

## Method 1: Finding true length

Swing the line parallel to the vertical or horizontal planes.

Here, the true length of AB is found by swinging it around so that it is parallel to the XY line and projecting it back into the elevation.

Alternatively, it can be found by swinging the elevation around so that it is parallel to the XY line and projecting it back into the plan, as shown here.

## Method 2: Finding the true length and angle of inclination

Fold the line flat onto the vertical or horizontal plane.

The alternative method shown here gives the true angle of inclination to the vertical plane.

This second alternative gives the true angle of inclination to the horizontal plane.

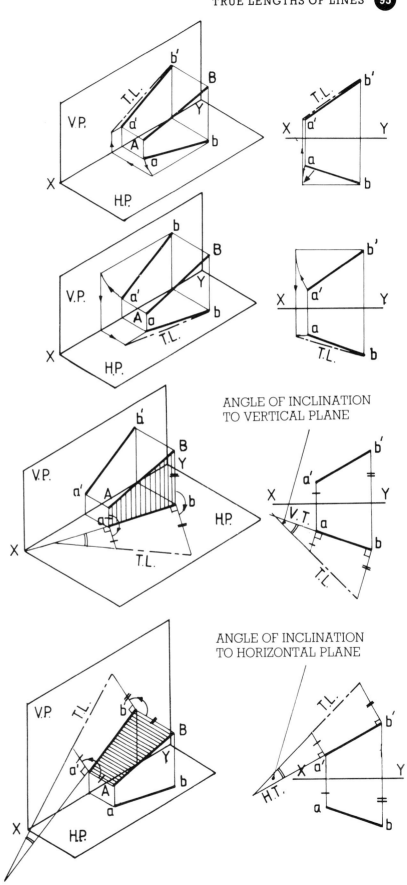

## PRACTICE 1

Each drawing shows the plan and elevation of a line (first angle protection). Determine the true length of the line and the angles of inclination to the vertical plane and horizontal plane in each case.

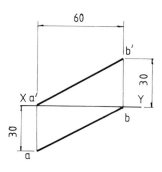

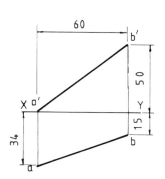

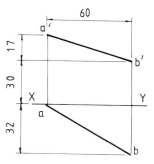

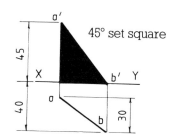

45° set square

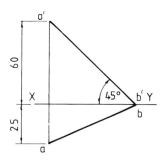

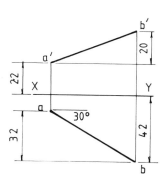

## PRACTICE 2

Orthographic drawings of two figures are given . Determine the true shape of each figure. (Find the true length of each side and construct the triangle.)

ELEVATION

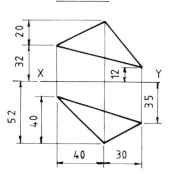

ELEVATION

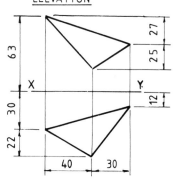

Solid geometry

## Development of surfaces

### Prisms

*Right triangular based prism:*

The height of each side is projected from the elevation and the length of each side is taken from the base.

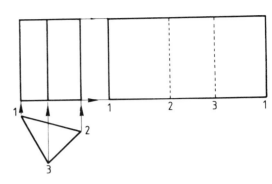

*Right triangular based prism cut by an inclined plane (PQ):*

Corners in the plan are numbered and sides are numbered in the development.
Lines are projected from the inclined plane.

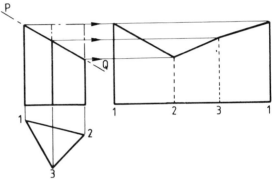

### Pyramids

*Square based right pyramid:*

Number all points. Line 01 in the development is parallel to edge 02 in the elevation.

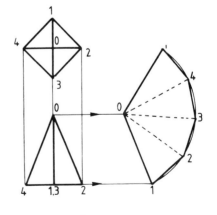

*Triangular based right truncated pyramid:*

End elevation gives true length of side 02. Line 03 is parallel to and equal in length to edge 02 in the elevation.
Project points as shown.

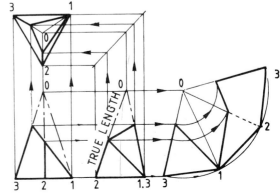

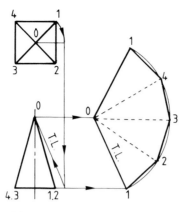

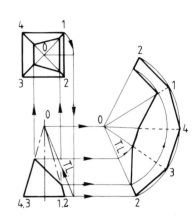

*Square based right pyramid:*

Determine true length (TL) of one edge as shown. Number all points. Line 01 (TL) in the development is parallel to TL in the elevation.

*Square based right truncated pyramid:*

Determine true length of edge 01. Line 02 in the development must be parallel to TL in the elevation. Project the points as shown.

## Prism and pyramid applications

The following drawings illustrate the use of pyramids for roofs of buildings. The sides are prisms.

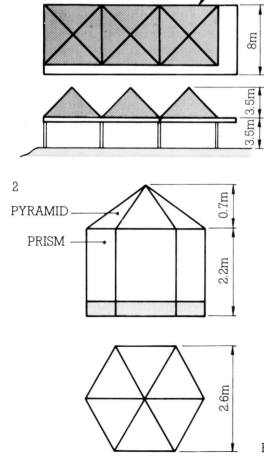

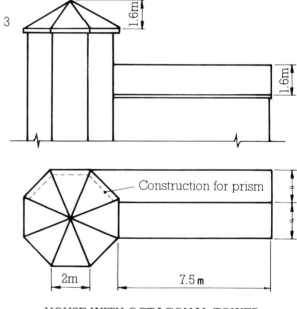

HOUSE WITH OCTAGONAL TOWER

FIRST ANGLE PROJECTION

## PRACTICE 1

Third angle views are given of the plan and elevation of the motor car showroom.

Draw to a scale of 1:100 the two given views. Add an end elevation looking from the right hand side of the front elevation. Use your own judgement where measurements are missing.

Use shading on your drawing.

## PRACTICE 2

To a scale of 1:20 draw these first angle views of the plan and elevation of a hexagonal greenhouse. Add an end elevation.

To the same scale draw a development of 2 sides and part of the top to determine the true shape of each side and the top.

Make an accurate isometric drawing of the green-house to a suitable scale.

## PRACTICE 3

The drawing in first angle projection is of the upper part of the building shown in the photograph, a house with an octagonal tower.

To a scale of 1:50 make an accurate orthographic drawing of the building and add two end elevations. Draw in the windows and shade your drawing. Only the essential measurements are given and you should use your own judgement where measurements have been omitted.

## PRACTICE 4

You will notice on the left hand side of the photograph the spire of a church. Make a pictorial freehand sketch of a church in your area. The church tower should have a spire.

# Developments relating to packaging

## PRACTICE 1

The photograph shows a die made out of cardboard.

Design a die or a game based on the development of the cube, given that each side is 80mm.

For a die the numbers on opposite sides will always add up to 7.

Use ink, coloured card or coloured pencil for your designs.

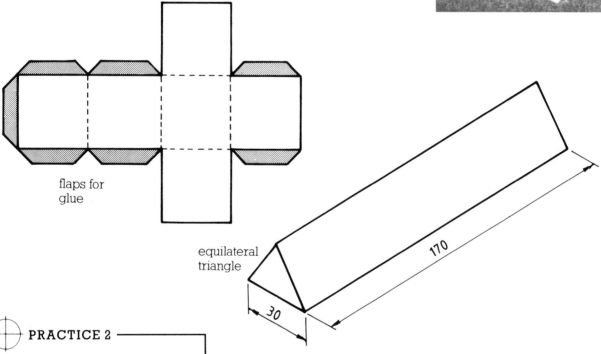

flaps for
glue

equilateral
triangle

30

170

## PRACTICE 2

The wrapper for the Toblerone bar shown in the photograph is a triangular prism made out of cardboard.

Draw on a sheet of manilla card a development of the prism, including the ends and the flap for glue. The tube can be opened from either end and is not sealed.

Cut out the development and make up the tube by glueing the flap and folding in the ends.

## PRACTICE 3

The container for the product shown in the photograph is made out of cardboard in the shape of a hexagonal prism.

1. Copy the isometric drawing shown, the end is a regular hexagon of sides 25mm. You will need to draw this as a separate view and transfer the measurements to the isometric drawing.
2. Draw a plan and two elevations of the container.
3. To a scale of full size, produce a complete development of the container including the flaps for glue. Cut out your development, fold it and make the container shown by glueing the flaps. The ends are closed.

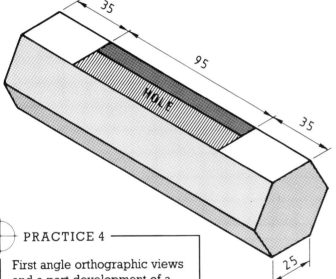

## PRACTICE 4

First angle orthographic views and a part development of a fruit juice container are shown.

1. To a scale of 1:2, draw the given orthographic views.
2. From your orthographic views draw a development of the sides and the bottom.
3. On both drawings devise and draw the arrangement for the top. It will be necessary for you to inspect a container similar to the one shown to enable you to work out the top.
4. Cut out, fold and glue the development including the top. Does your arrangement for the top work?

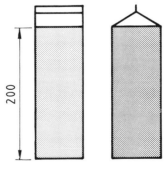

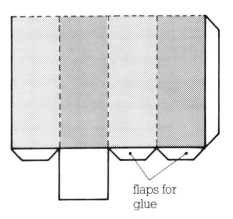

flaps for glue

## PRACTICE 5

The drawings show the plan, elevations and part development for the container in the photograph.

1. Using A2 paper, draw the given views and a complete development including the top and bottom.
2. Make a model from your development.
3. By means of freehand sketches, design some method of keeping the orange (⌀60) centrally positioned inside the container.

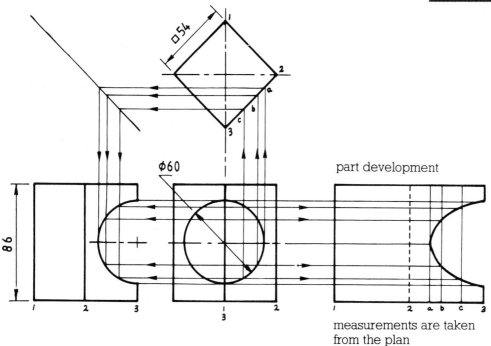

part development

measurements are taken from the plan

⌀60

□54

86

## PRACTICE 6

The inverted plan and front elevation of the container in the photograph are shown. For the purpose of this drawing the top and bottom are flat.

1. To a scale of full size, draw the given views using A2 paper and an end elevation viewed from the right hand side of the front elevation. Include the hole.
2. Draw a development of the sides, top and bottom of the container.
3. Cut out your development and make a model of the container.

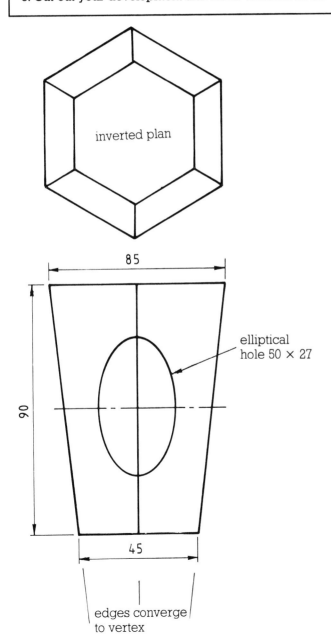

inverted plan

85

elliptical hole 50 × 27

90

45

edges converge to vertex

## Cylinders

*Right cylinder:*

The height of the development is projected from the elevation and the length of the development equals the circumference of the cylinder. (Circumference = $2\pi r$).

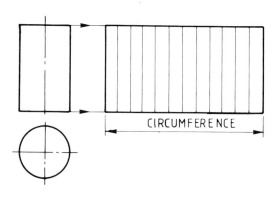

*Right cylinder cut by inclined plane (PQ):*

The plan is divided into twelve equal parts and the circumference in the development is divided into twelve equal parts. Lines are numbered and projected as shown.

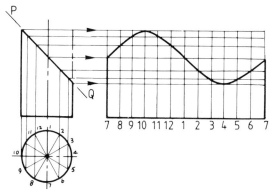

## Cones

*Right cone:*

Line 0–1 in the development is parallel to the side of the cone.

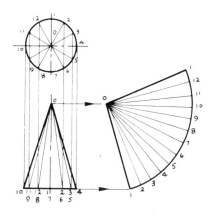

*Right truncated cone:*

Line 0–10 in the development is parallel to the side of the cone.

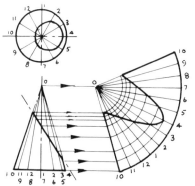

# Models using developments

⊕ PRACTICE 1 ─────────────────

To a scale of 1:50 draw the plan and elevation of the tower shown here, given that the base is square and of sides 3 metres.

To the same scale draw a development and make a cardboard model of the tower. Add shading and other details if you wish.

⊕ PRACTICE 2 ─────────────────

The photograph shows a cylindrical tower and a conical roof. The height of the cylinder is 3 metres and its diameter is 2.5 metres. The height of the conical roof is 3 metres.

Draw to a scale of 1:50 the plan and elevation of the tower. Draw a development and make a model of the tower and roof.

# Curves and lines of intersection

As a general rule sections are taken through the drawing to determine the positions of points on the intersection.

*Cylinders of same Ø at right angles:*
Semicircles are constructed and numbered as shown.

Lines are projected from the plan to give points on the line of intersection.

When both cylinders are of the same diameter and on the same centre lines, the line of intersection will be a straight line.

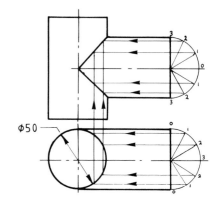

φ50

*Cylinders of same Ø at 60°:*
The given view shows the elliptical end of the cylinder in the plan.

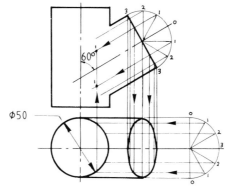

φ50

## PRACTICE 1

Copy the drawing, and complete the elevation showing the line of intersection.

*Cylinders of different Ø at 45°:*
The given view shows the curve of intersection in the elevation.

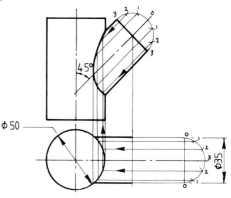

φ50

φ35

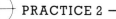

## PRACTICE 2

Copy the elevation and complete the plan showing the elliptical end of the cylinder.

*Cylinders of different Ø at 90°:*
Plan and elevation are shown.

## PRACTICE 3

Draw the given views and complete the elevation by showing the curve of the intersection.

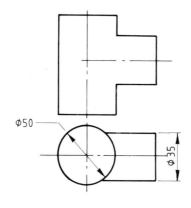

φ50

φ35

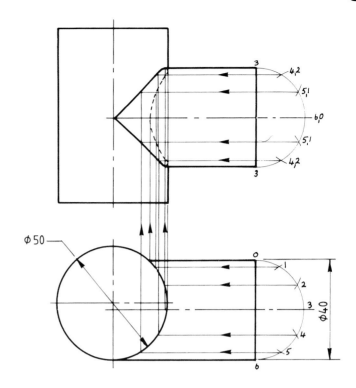

*Two off-set cylinders:*

The numbering of the points on the construction is to avoid confusion with the hidden detail.

---

### PRACTICE 4

Copy the drawing using the construction shown.

---

*Cylinder and square prism:*

Horizontal sections are taken at convenient points in the end elevation to enable points to be located on the curve of intersection.

The isometric drawing shows one such section.

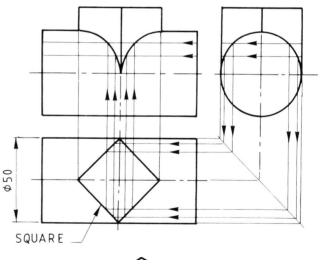

---

### PRACTICE 5

Draw this example, using the measurements given.

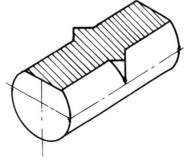

*Square prism and triangular prism:*

The plan, elevation and end elevation are needed for this construction. All corners are projected from the plan and end elevation into the elevation. Any point on the drawing can be projected through all the views to its starting point.

 **PRACTICE 6**

Copy the drawing using your own sizes for the prisms.

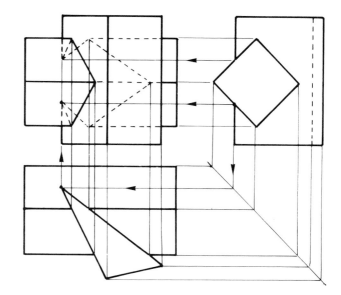

*Cone and cylinder:*

The three views are drawn and horizontal sections are taken in the end elevation at convenient points. Lines are projected around the drawing to give points on the curve of intersection in the plan and elevation.

The isometric drawing shows one such section.

 **PRACTICE 7**

Draw this example using the measurements given.

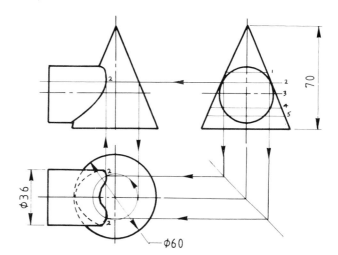

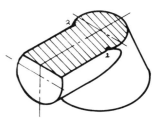

*Cone and sphere:*

Horizontal sections are taken through the elevation and projected into the plan and end elevation. Several sections are taken at convenient positions to obtain points on the curve. The projection of one such section is shown in detail.

 **PRACTICE 8** ───────

Make an accurate copy of this drawing showing all the construction.

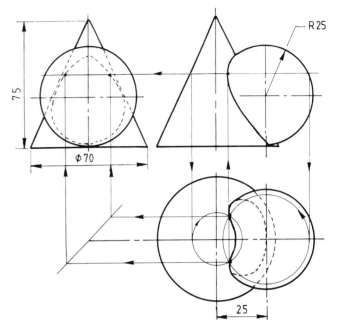

*Link:*

The drawing shows three views of a junction piece made from rectangular and round section material.

The curve of intersection is obtained by taking horizontal sections at convenient positions through the elevation.

The projection of one such section is shown, giving points on the curve of intersection in the elevations. Several sections are taken to give points for a complete curve.

 **PRACTICE 9** ───────

Make an accurate copy of this drawing showing all the construction.

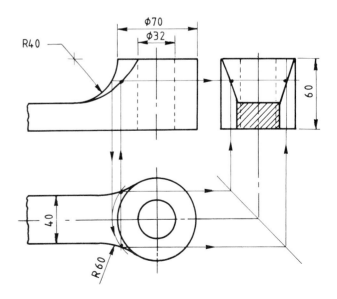

# Auxiliary views

Auxiliary views, or elevations are taken when the object is viewed from a direction other than the conventional plan and elevations. In the example below the object has been viewed from one corner and lines are projected back from the plan to give an auxiliary elevation. Heights for the auxiliary elevation are taken from the front elevation.

Auxiliary views are useful to show additional details of drawings and to determine the true shape of certain surfaces.

## Worked example 1

▼ Auxiliary elevation viewed from the direction of arrow A.

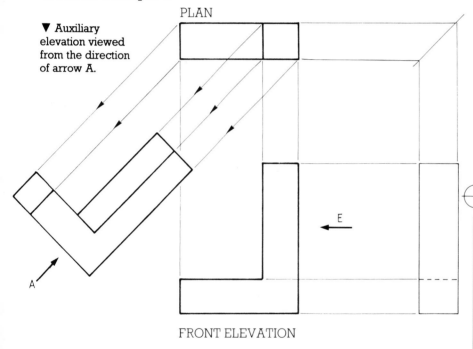

PLAN

FRONT ELEVATION

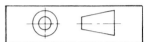

---

⊕ **PRACTICE 2**

Draw the front elevation and plan as shown in the drawing below.

1. Project and end elevation as indicated by letter E.
2. Project an auxiliary elevation as seen from the direction of arrow A. Show hidden edges.

---

⊕ **PRACTICE 1**

Draw in third angle projection the front elevation, plan and auxiliary elevation plan as shown above. Use your own measurements.

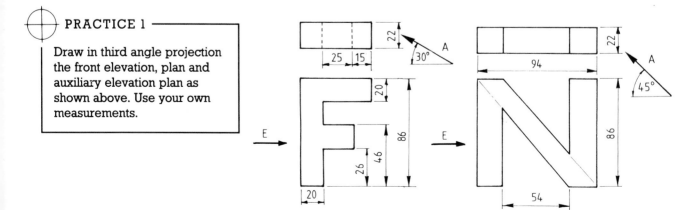

# Worked example 2

In this drawing, the front elevation is viewed from the direction of
arrow A to give an auxiliary plan.

Procedure:
Project lines from the nearest edge of the front elevation and work
backwards. Measurements for width are stepped off from the plan.

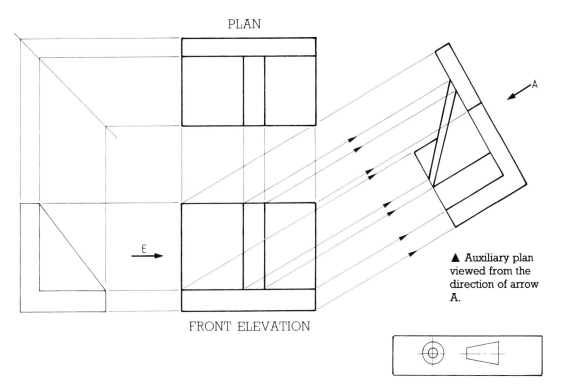

PLAN

E

FRONT ELEVATION

▲ Auxiliary plan
viewed from the
direction of arrow
A.

## PRACTICE 3

For each example draw the front elevation and plan
as shown in third angle projection.
1. Project an end elevation as indicated by
   arrow E.
2. Project an auxiliary plan viewed from the
   direction of arrow A. Show hidden edges.

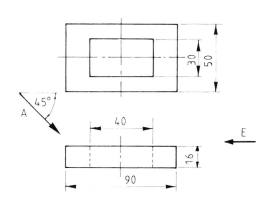

A 45°

30 50

40

90

16

E

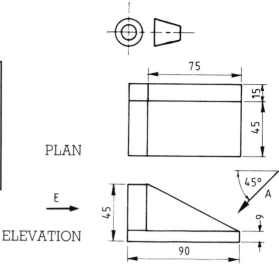

**PRACTICE 4**

Draw the plan and front elevation in third angle projection as shown.

1. Project an end elevation as indicated by arrow E.
2. Project an auxiliary plan as viewed from the direction of arrow A.

PLAN

E

ELEVATION

## Worked example 3

This drawing shows the procedure for dealing with curves.

Construction lines (a, b, c) are drawn in the front elevation at convenient intervals. They are projected into the plan and into the auxiliary elevation. Heights from the front elevation are stepped off on each line.

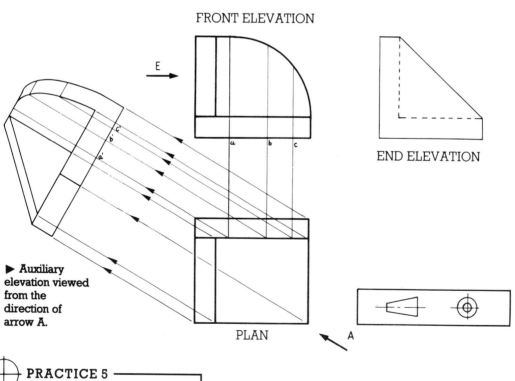

FRONT ELEVATION

E

END ELEVATION

▶ Auxiliary elevation viewed from the direction of arrow A.

PLAN        A

**PRACTICE 5**

Make a copy of this drawing using your own measurements for the plan and front elevation.

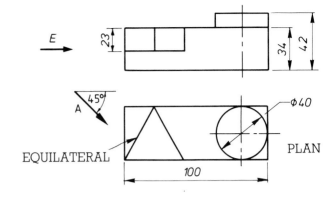

## PRACTICE 6

Draw the front elevation and plan in first angle projection.

1. Project an end elevation as indicated by arrow E.
2. Project an auxiliary elevation viewed from the direction of arrow A.

EQUILATERAL

PLAN

FRONT ELEVATION

## PRACTICE 7

Draw the front elevation and end elevation in first angle projection as shown.

1. Project a plan as indicated by arrow P.
2. Project an auxiliary plan viewed from the direction of arrow A.

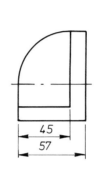

# Conic sections

True shapes of surfaces are found by projecting lines at right angles to the cutting plane in a similar way to drawing an auxiliary view.

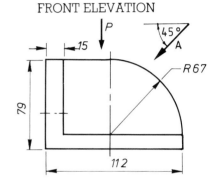

CUTTING
PLANE
VERTICAL

ELEVATION
TRUE SHAPE-
HYPERBOLA

The true shape of the section cut by an inclined plane parallel to one side of the cone will be a parabola, as shown in the drawing here.

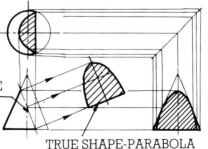

CUTTING PLANE
PARALLEL TO
ONE SIDE

TRUE SHAPE-PARABOLA

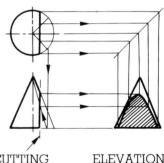

TRUE SHAPE-
ELLIPSE

CUTTING
PLANE CUTS
BOTH SIDES

The true shape of the section cut by the inclined plane will be an ellipse. The inclined plane must cut both sides of the cone, as the drawing shows.

## Symbols and conventions

The symbols and conventions shown here are based on British Standards Publication No. 308 *Engineering Drawing Practice*.

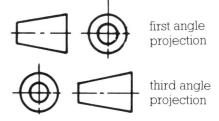

first angle projection

third angle projection

round shaft with square end

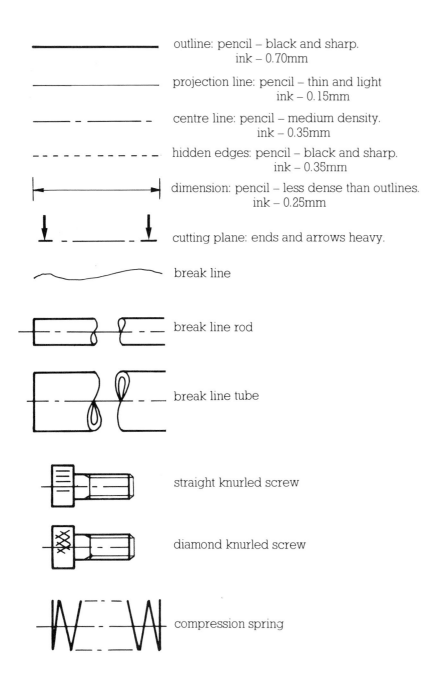

outline: pencil – black and sharp.
ink – 0.70mm

projection line: pencil – thin and light
ink – 0.15mm

centre line: pencil – medium density.
ink – 0.35mm

hidden edges: pencil – black and sharp.
ink – 0.35mm

dimension: pencil – less dense than outlines.
ink – 0.25mm

cutting plane: ends and arrows heavy.

break line

break line rod

break line tube

straight knurled screw

diamond knurled screw

compression spring

## Abbreviations

| | |
|---|---|
| $\phi$ | diameter |
| □ | square |
| PCD | pitch circle diameter |
| PCR | pitch circle radius |
| CRS | centres |
| A/C | across the corners |
| A/F | across the flats |
| CSK | countersunk |
| C'BORE | counterbore |
| S'FACE | spotface |
| mm | millimetres |
| m | metres |
| Km | kilometres |
| M | ISO metric thread |

# Electrical/electronic appliances

 PRACTICE 1

This isometric drawing is a simplified version of the micro-processor shown in the photograph.

Draw on a sheet of A2 paper the following:

1. An isometric drawing as shown. Shading can be used.
2. A front elevation.
3. An end elevation.
4. A plan.

Your drawing should be to a scale of full size and only the essential measurements are given. Use your own judgement where measurements have been omitted.

The layout for the keyboard has not been shown. From one of the computers in your school, find out the correct layout for the keyboard and draw it into the space in your plan.

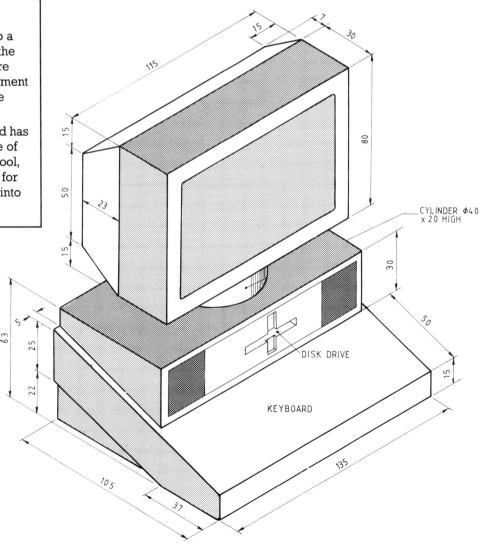

## PRACTICE 2

The isometric drawing shows a simplified version of the micrometer in the photograph. Not all the dimensions have been given; small radii should be 3mm or 5mm, and radii indicated by R can be worked out. Other measurements not given should be estimated.

Draw on a sheet of A3 paper to a scale of full size the following views:

1. A front elevation.
2. An end elevation viewed from the left hand side of the front elevation.
3. A plan.

Do not show any hidden edges. Insert ten dimensions, print a title block & indicate the projection used.

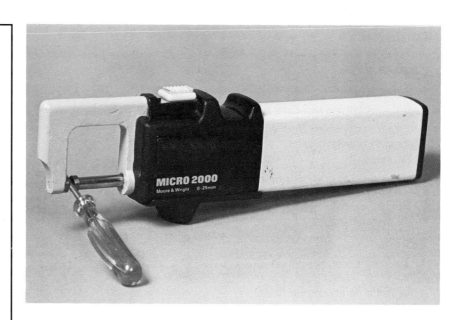

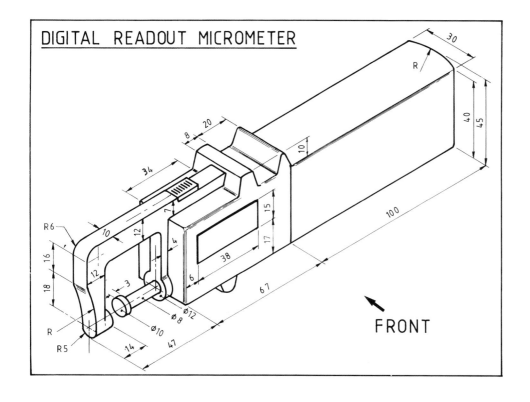

DIGITAL READOUT MICROMETER

FRONT

# Assembly drawing (1)

⊕ PRACTICE 1 ─────────────────────────────

Freehand sketches of the outer case of the fluorescent camping lantern in the photograph are drawn below.

1. With all the parts assembled in their correct positions (see photograph), draw to a scale of full size the following views:
   A front elevation as indicated by the arrow.
   A plan.
   An end elevation viewed from the right hand side of the front elevation.

   Insert six important dimensions on your drawing.
   Do not show hidden edges.

2. Make a freehand pictorial sketch of the assembled lantern. Include the lamp, reflector and switch.
   Use shading or colour.

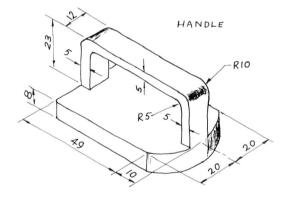

HANDLE

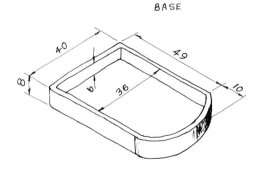

BASE

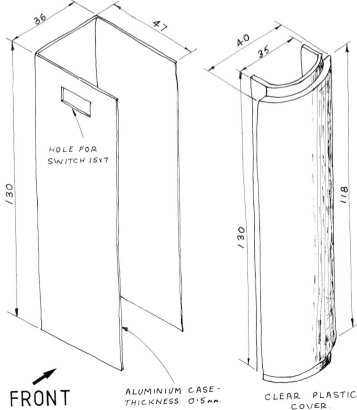

FRONT

HOLE FOR SWITCH 15x7

ALUMINIUM CASE-
THICKNESS 0.5 mm.

CLEAR PLASTIC
COVER.

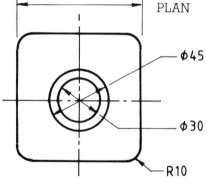

## Sectional views

Sectional views are used to show inside details of objects more clearly.

The drawings below show (in simplified isometric form) the spindle housing illustrated in the photograph.

1. The shaded area and the centre line show the cutting plane for the section. The position of the sectional on view is indicated by the of direction of the arrows A – A.

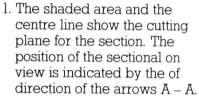

2. The part of the object *behind* the arrows is removed in a sectional view. Some hidden edges now become visible and they are drawn on outlines.

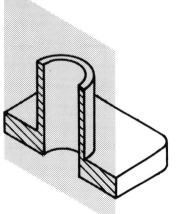

3. The section is shaded or cross-hatched with lines angled at 45° and approximately 4mm apart. The sectional view is labelled – in this case A – A, according to the cutting plane in the front elevation.

PRACTICE 1

Make a accurate copy of this orthographic drawing. Use A3 paper.

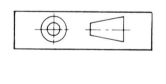

PLAN

□ 90

φ 45

φ 30

R10

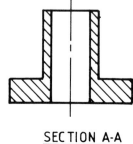

SECTION A-A

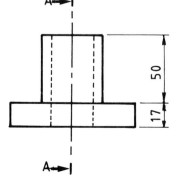

50

17

## PRACTICE 2

The orthographic drawings show the plan, front elevation and a sectional end elevation of the soap tray in isometric projection.

Make an accurate copy of the soap tray in orthographic projection. The thickness of all the plastic is 3mm. Assume any dimensions not given. The drawing shown is in third angle projection, your drawing should be in first angle projection.

By means of freehand isometric sketches of approximately full size design a suitable fitment to enable the soap tray to be attached to the wall. The soap tray will fit onto the attachment if pushed downwards in the direction of arrow P.

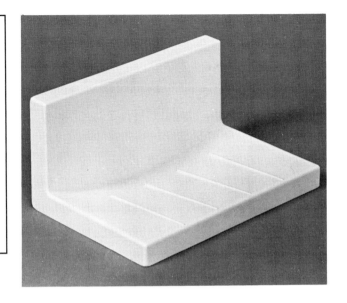

SOAP TRAY

P

135

X

12

50

75

12

4 RIDGES
EQUISPACED

X

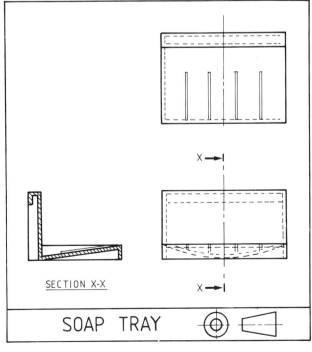

X

X

SECTION X-X

X

SOAP TRAY

## Sectional views of ribs

Ribs or webs are used in castings and mouldings to give additional support and strength to an object.

> The following rules apply to sections taken through ribs:
> 1. If the rib is cut longitudinally, in the section it is shown as an outside view (see drawing A).
> 2. If the cutting plane is across the rib, it is shown in section (see drawing B).
> 3. Hidden edges are not usually shown in sectional views.

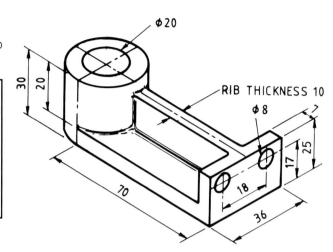

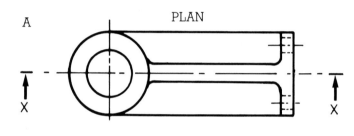

A PLAN          B PLAN

SECTION Y-Y

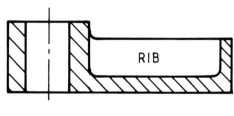

RIB

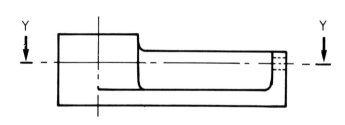

SECTION X-X

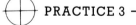 PRACTICE 3

On the left hand side of a sheet of A3 paper, draw the following views:
A sectional front elevation through cutting plane X – X;
A sectional plan through cutting plane Y – Y;
An end elevation viewed from the right hand side of the front elevation.

Indicate the cutting planes and label the sections on your drawing.

To a scale of 1½ × full size make an accurate isometric drawing of the bracket on the right hand side of the paper.

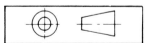

 PRACTICE 4 ─────────────────────────

For these two isometric drawings draw:

A front elevation as indicated by arrow Y.

A sectional elevation through cutting plane X – X.

A plan in projection with the front elevation.

Show hidden detail in the plan only, and add six dimensions to your drawing. Indicate the projection and the scale in your title block.

ROCKER BEARING          SLIDING BRACKET

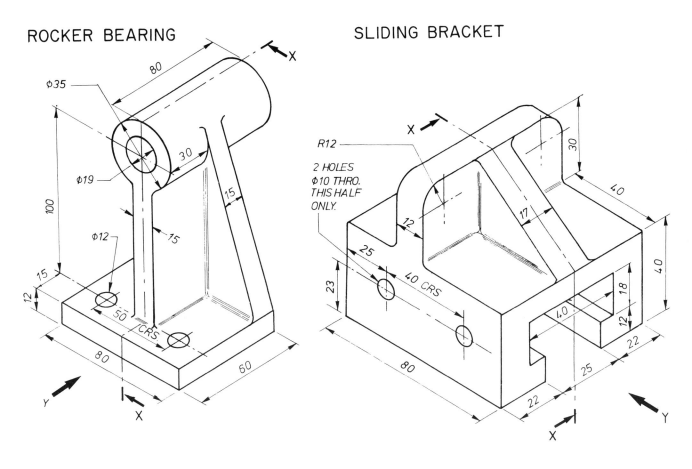

## Screwed fixings

The drawings show the method of drawing a screw thread in a sectional view.

The views here are in third angle projection.

> **Metric thread measurements:**
> **Example: M20 × 2, 30 long. This means a metric thread whose outside diameter is 20mm, pitch is 2mm and the thread is 30mm long.**

*Hole drilled for tapping:*
The diameter of this hole will be the diameter of the thread minus the pitch.

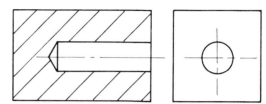

*Tapped hole:*
The diameter of the broken circle is the diameter of the thread. It is not possible to cut the thread to the bottom of the hole.

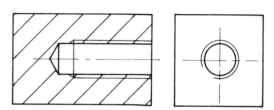

*Knurled screw:*
The same rules apply concerning the diameters of the threads.

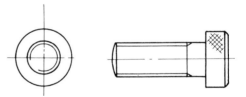

*Tapped hole and knurled screw:*
The knurled screw is not sectioned, and where the two threads are in contact section lines are not shown.

In a non-section drawing the threaded parts would be shown hidden, using dotted lines.

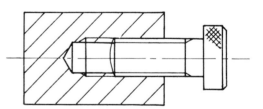

*Machine screws:*
The sectional drawing shows the elevations of some of the most common machine screws. The end of the screw does not normally fit to the end of the tapped hole.

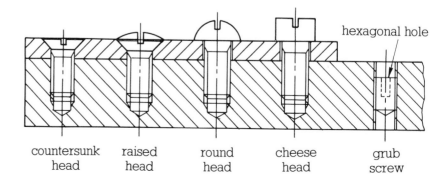

hexagonal hole

| countersunk head | raised head | round head | cheese head | grub screw |

## PRACTICE 5

The drawing shows the plan and elevation of a perspex pepper mill drawn in third angle projection.

On a sheet of A3 paper arranged vertically, draw to a scale of 1½ × full size the following views:

1. The plan and elevation as shown.
2. A sectional elevation, the direction of the section being indicated by cutting plane A – A.
3. Insert ten dimensions on your drawing.
4. Draw a suitable title block.

The spherical knob is attached to the shaft by means of a M5 thread.

The pepper mill mechanism has been shown as a shaded area and you should show this in a similar way. If you wish, you can sketch some peppercorns in the sectional view.

Assume any dimensions not given.

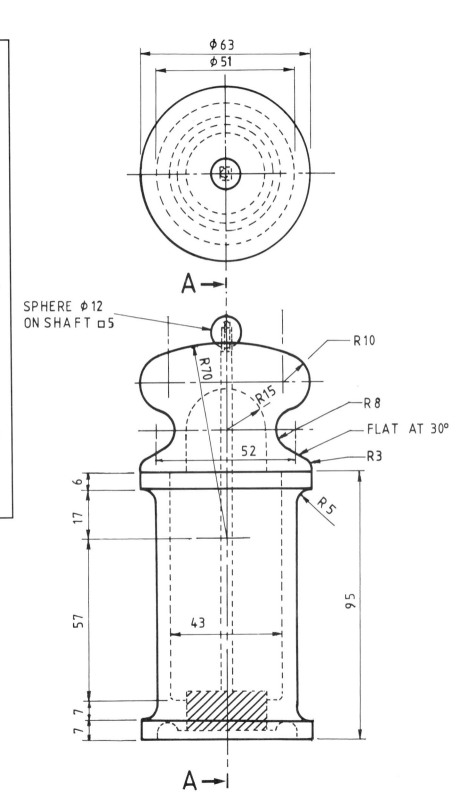

## Assembly drawing (2)

The various parts of a lathe tool holder are shown in the orthographic drawings.

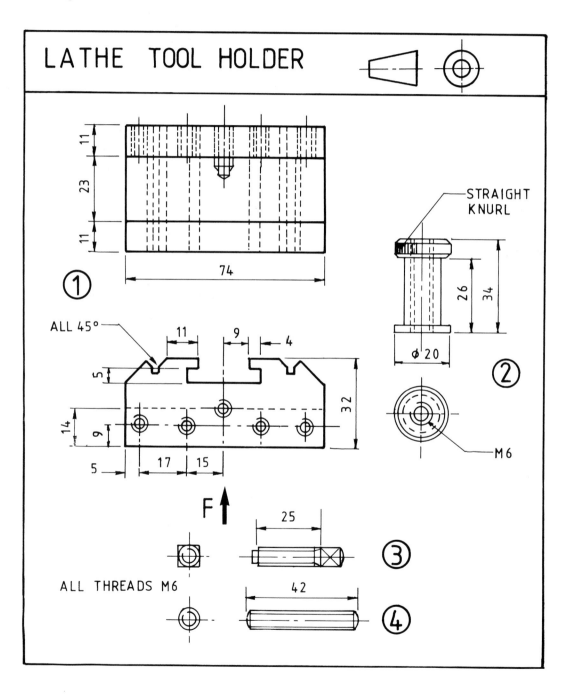

| PART NO. | NAME | NO. OFF |
|----------|------|---------|
| 1 | Body | 1 |
| 2 | Adjuster | 1 |
| 3 | Square head bolt | 5 |
| 4 | Stud | 1 |

The parts list above indicates the number off of each part.

 PRACTICE 1

With all the parts assembled, draw on A3 paper, the following views to a scale of full size:
1. A plan.
2. A sectional front view in the direction of arrow F. The plane of the section is the centre line passing through the four screw threads.
3. An end elevation viewed from the left hand side of the front view.
4. Fully dimension your drawing, add a title block and state the projection used.

Note the following points:
The convention used for straight knurling (Part 2).
Diagonals to indicate a square head and the thread is undercut to prevent it becoming damaged when it is tightened onto the lathe tool (Part 3).
Use your own judgement where dimensions have been omitted.

## PRACTICE 2

The third angle orthographic drawings show the various components of an electric buzzer which can be made in the school workshop. The isometric drawing shows the components assembled, and the dotted line shows the wiring of the buzzer.

Draw to a scale of full size, with all the parts assembled, orthographic views as follows:

1. A plan.
2. A sectional front elevation, the section being taken through the centre of the coil assembly.
3. An end elevation viewed from the right hand side of the front elevation.

Use a suitable method for fixing parts D, E and H to the 12mm thick perspex base. Assume any measurements not given.

Sketch a freehand pictorial view of the complete assembly. Use colour and shading.

Draw a circuit diagram of the arrangement including a 6 volt battery and bell push. The circuit breaker can be shown as a switch.

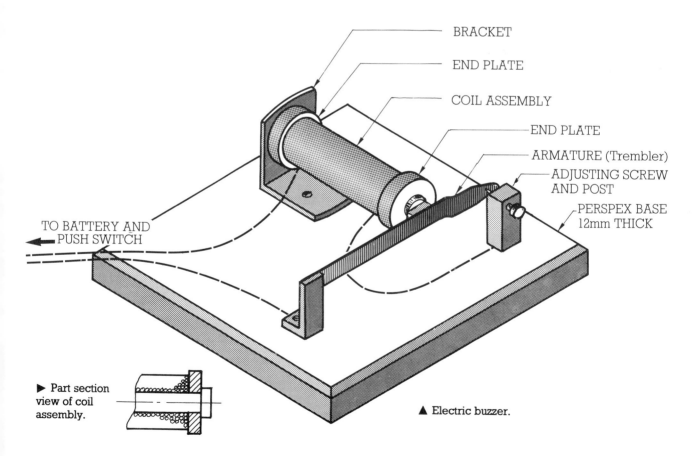

BRACKET

END PLATE

COIL ASSEMBLY

END PLATE

ARMATURE (Trembler)

ADJUSTING SCREW AND POST

PERSPEX BASE 12mm THICK

TO BATTERY AND PUSH SWITCH

▶ Part section view of coil assembly.

▲ Electric buzzer.

| PART | NAME | MATERIAL |
|------|------|----------|
| A | End plate | Perspex |
| B | Core | Soft iron |
| C | End plate | Perspex |
| D | Bracket | Mild steel |
| E | Armature | Spring steel |
| F | Spring | Spring steel |
| G | Adjusting screw | Brass |
| H | Post | Brass |

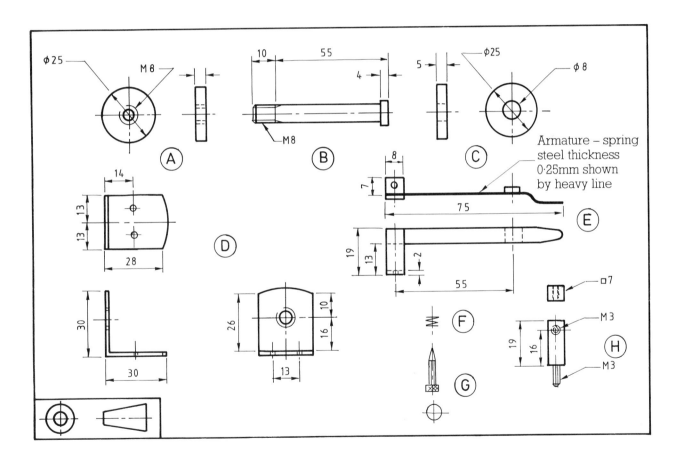

PART SECTION Y-Y

VIEWS OF THE BACK

TOP

walls
thickness 2

pin ⌀3

2 holes ⌀6

35

15

5

33

4 8

33

18

14

Y

Y

BOTTOM

R5

10

74

74

74

34

74

24

12

2

10

⌀19

⌀16

spigot ⌀6
tapped hole ⌀3

post ⌀6
hole ⌀3

2 holes ⌀3

2 pins ⌀3 2 pins ⌀2

2 pins ⌀3

96

X

X

FRONT ELEVATION
HALF SECTION X-X

12

19

4

2

⌀19

SELF TAPPING
SCREWS M4 ×
6 long
4 off

34 CRS

9

TENSION PAD
heavy line shows
spring 0·5mm thick

⌀2

6

⌀10

10

ROLLER
2 off

⌀19

10

⌀34

SPOOL
2 off

## PRACTICE 3

Third angle orthographic views of the various parts of a music cassette (slightly modified) are given.

With all the parts assembled in their correct positions, draw to a scale of full size the following views:

A plan, the left hand half being a view with the top removed.

A front elevation, the left hand half being a section through centre line X – X (include the top). Refer to page 137 on half sections.

An end elevation.

A view of the back.

A parts list indicating the number off of each part. Do not include any hidden edges or dimensions. Assume any dimension not given.

If you are able to obtain an old and useless cassette, dismantle it to find the correct position for the various parts. Do *not* dismantle a new cassette – you will ruin it!

Refer to pages 13–141 on half sections.

# Nut and bolt proportions

The drawing shows the proportions for the hexagon nut and bolt.

D refers to the outside diameter of the bolt. For example, M20 means a metric thread where D is 20mm.

The length of the thread and the length of the bolt will depend on its application.

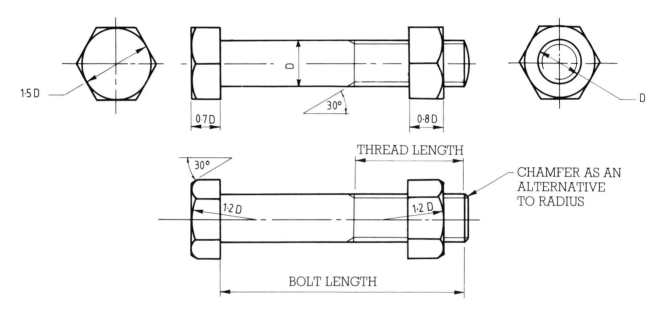

## The nut and bolt in sectional views

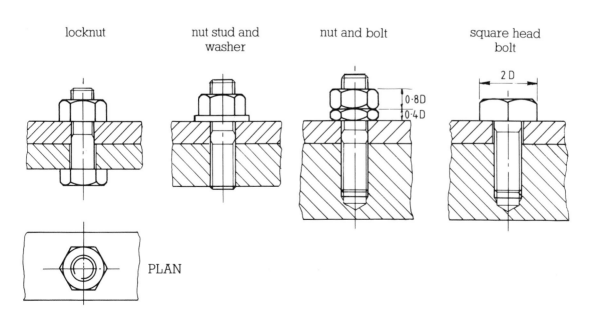

locknut     nut stud and washer     nut and bolt     square head bolt

PLAN

▲ Lathe
tool post.

## Sections of nuts, bolts and screw threads

The first angle orthographic drawing illustrates the following rules
concerning screw threads in section:

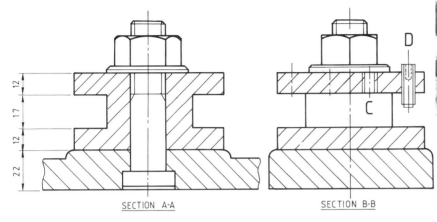

SECTION A-A         SECTION B-B

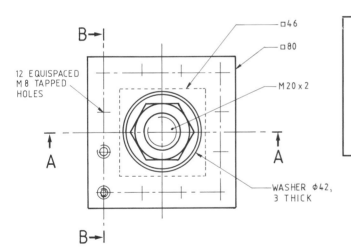

1. A bolt is shown as an outside view.
2. A nut is shown as an outside view.
3. A washer is shown as an outside view.
4. Part C, a tapped hole, the cross-hatching covers
   the thread.
5. Part D, the hexagon slot grub screw. When a
   threaded bolt or screw is fitted into a tapped hole
   the thread is not cross-hatched.

---

⊕ PRACTICE 1 ————————————————

Draw to a scale of full size on A3 paper the following views of the lathe
tool post:
The plan , sectional front elevation and sectional end elevation.
Fully label the sectional views and the cutting planes.

### CROSS HATCHING

The drawing consists of two separate parts, the tool post and the cross
slide (not drawn in the plan). To show this clearly the cross-hatching is
drawn in opposite directions.

The photograph and drawing show the base for an office swivel chair. Note the following points:

1. Pentagon construction: Refer to page 5 for the construction of the pentagon.
2. Tangency: The feet are tangents to two circles of diameter 32 and 40. You should accurately draw in the circles. The straight lines for the legs can then be drawn in. There is no need to use a construction.
3. Knob: The tapped hole at B is for a tightening device which consists of a diameter 8 rod which is threaded at one end and has a knob fixed to the other end (see photograph).
4. Break line: C shows the use of a break line in a tube to shorten the stem. This enables it to fit onto the drawing.
5. Revolved section: A revolved section at D shows the cross-sectional shape of the leg at the position where it is drawn.
6. Spring: The symbol for a compression spring is shown at E. On a larger drawing the spring (or part of it) could be drawn accurately. Refer to pages 56–58 on the helix.
7. Hidden edges for only one leg have been shown. This has been done for the purpose of clarity. Because each leg is the same, it would be reasonable to assume that the hidden detail at D is the same for each leg.

⊕ PRACTICE 2 ───────────────

To a scale of full size, on A2 paper, with one castor in position, draw the following views:

A plan and elevation as shown.

An end elevation. This should be a sectional view, the cutting plane of the section being indicated by A – A. The castor should be positioned in the leg marked D.

As an additional exercise you could draw the helical spring in position in the sectioned view. The dimensions for the round sectioned spring are as follows: outside ⌀ 54mm, cross section of spring ⌀ 6, pitch 36mm.

By means of freehand sketches, design a suitable knob to fit at B. Make an orthographic drawing of the knob and screwed shaft.

Label and dimension your drawings, insert a title block and projection.

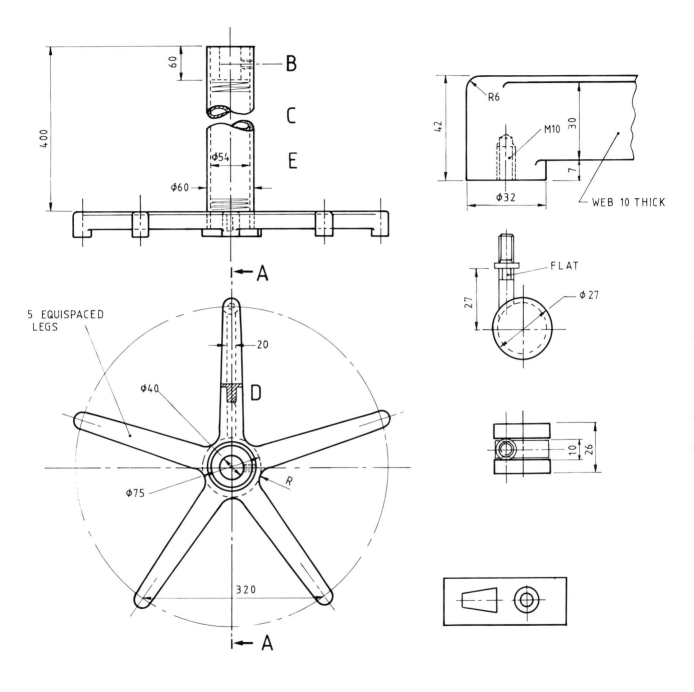

The photograph and drawings show the base and motor for a liquidiser. Note the following points:

1. Dimensions: The symbol for the square base has been used in the plan.
2. Splined wheel: The shape is only partly shown and it is assumed that it will be the same all round. There are 12 serrations.
3. Shading: The motor position is shown as a shaded area. The actual workings of the motor are not drawn in. Separate drawings would be needed for the motor detail.

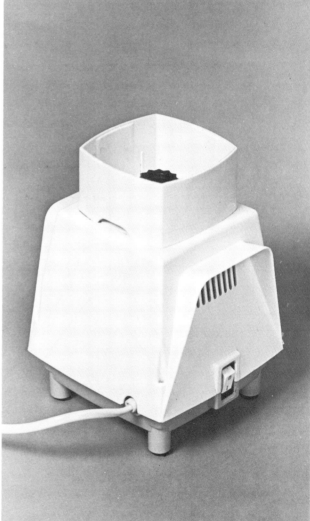

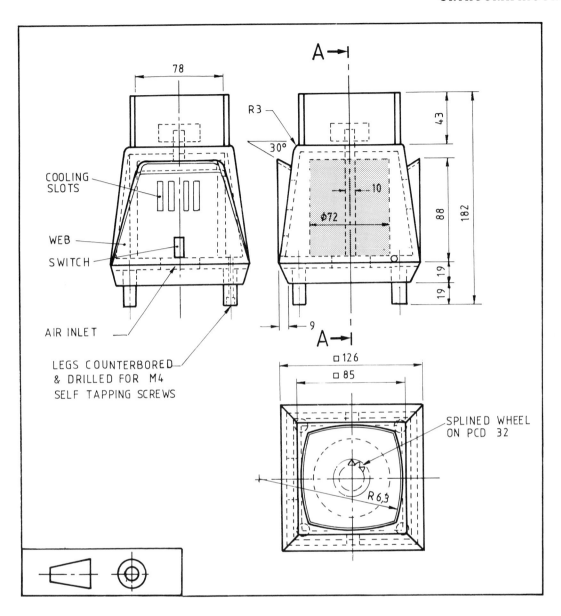

A → |

78

R3

30°

COOLING
SLOTS

WEB

SWITCH

AIR INLET

LEGS COUNTERBORED
& DRILLED FOR M4
SELF TAPPING SCREWS

43

10

φ72

88

182

19

19

19

9

A → |

□ 126

□ 85

SPLINED WHEEL
ON PCD 32

R 6,3

---

⊕ PRACTICE 3 ─────────

To a scale of full size, on A2 paper and in third angle
projection, draw the following views:

A plan.
A front elevation.
A sectional end elevation, the plane of the section
and the direction of the view being indicated by
A – A.

Show hidden edges in the plan and front elevation
only and add ten dimensions to your drawing.
Assume any measurements not given.

⊕ PRACTICE 4 ─────────

Draw a circuit diagram of the
arrangement starting from a 13
amp plug. Use the symbol
shown below for the motor.

Ⓜ   motor

## Sections of shafts and keyways

The following rules apply to sections of shafts and keyways:

1. The shaft is drawn as an outside view.
2. The keyway in this example is shown as hidden detail.
3. The key is shown as an outside view.

▲ Motor and pulley of a small bandsaw.

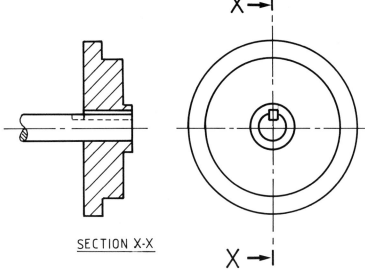

SECTION X-X

PRACTICE 5

Make an exploded freehand pictorial sketch of the motor shaft, key and pulley.

## Half sections

The first angle orthographic drawing of the plan and elevation of a guide for a power hacksaw vice screw is an example of a half section.

When an object is symmetrical, a half section is a useful method of giving additional detail on the same view. The half section should be fully labelled.

*Note:* The drawing of the plan shows details only of the guide. The base onto which it is fixed is not fully drawn.

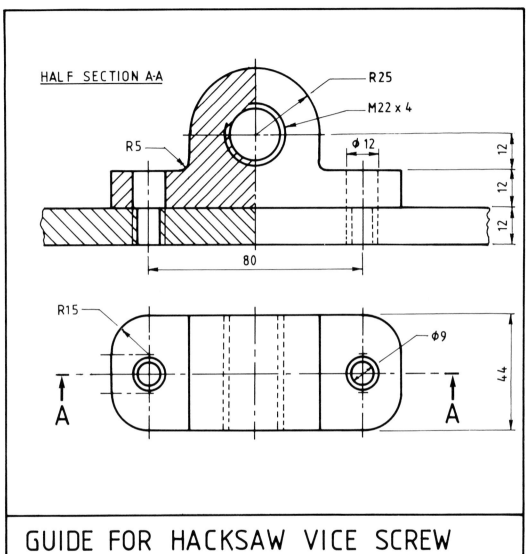

HALF SECTION A·A

R25

M22 x 4

R5

φ 12

12

12

12

80

R15

φ9

44

A    A

GUIDE FOR HACKSAW VICE SCREW

⊕ PRACTICE 6

Draw the given views and an end elevation. Insert suitable bolts and washers in the holes.

Make a full size pictorial (isometric or oblique) drawing of the guide only.

**138** GRAPHICAL COMMUNICATION 2

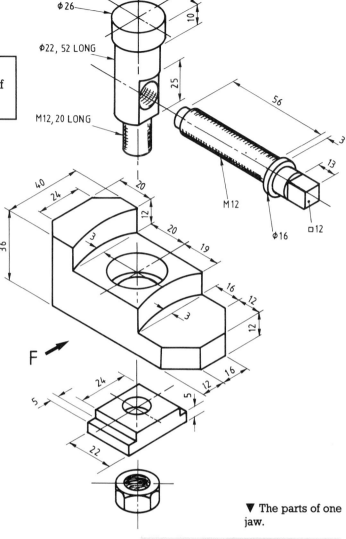

## PRACTICE 7

The exploded isometric drawing shows one jaw of the four jaw face plate in the photograph.

▲ Four jaw face plate.

▼ The parts of one jaw.

You are required to draw on A3 paper in orthographic projection the following views of the fully assembled jaw, to a scale of full size:

1. A sectional front elevation viewed from the direction of arrow F. The section being taken through the centre of the object. In this view you will only cross hatch the body and the clamping piece.
2. A plan.
3. Two end views, one viewed from the left hand side and the other viewed from the right hand side of the front view.

Show hidden edges in the plan only and assume any dimensions not given.

Add six dimensions to your drawing. These should be of a varied nature eg. a radius, a diameter, a screw thread, an angle or a length.

Print a title block and state the projection used.

▶ Assembled jaw.

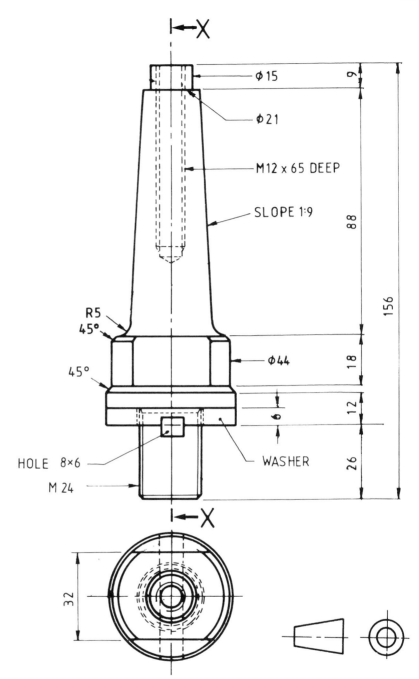

ø 15

ø 21

M12 x 65 DEEP

SLOPE 1:9

R5
45°

45°

ø 44

HOLE 8×6

M 24

WASHER

9

88

156

18

12

26

32

## PRACTICE 8

The photograph and ortho-
graphic drawings show a chuck
for holding milling tools on a
vertical milling machine.

Draw to a scale or full size the
following views in orthographic
projection:

1. The front elevation and plan
   as shown.
2. A half sectional end elevation
   the direction of the required
   view and the plane of the
   section being indicated by
   centre line X – X.

Use your own judgement where
measurements have been
omitted.

Print ten important dimensions
on your drawing and add a title
block stating the projection
used.

## PRACTICE 9

Make a full size pictorial sketch
of the milling tool holder.
Shading can be used.

The drawings below show some of the methods of fixing shafts, bolts and pulleys.

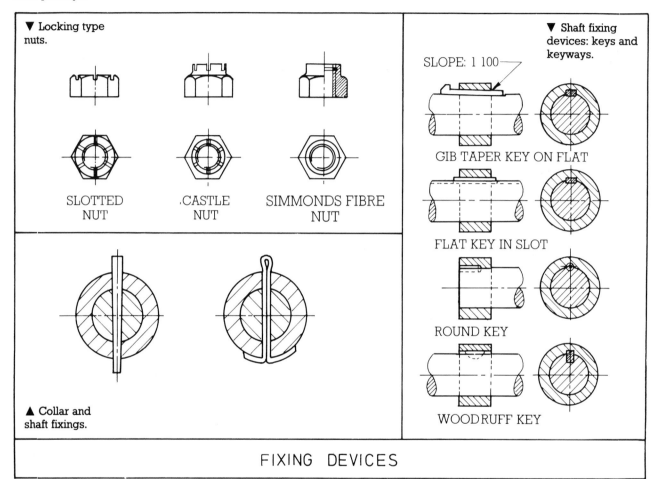

▼ Locking type nuts.

SLOTTED NUT    .CASTLE NUT    SIMMONDS FIBRE NUT

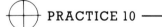
▲ Collar and shaft fixings.

▼ Shaft fixing devices: keys and keyways.

SLOPE: 1 100

GIB TAPER KEY ON FLAT

FLAT KEY IN SLOT

ROUND KEY

WOODRUFF KEY

FIXING DEVICES

---

⊕ PRACTICE 10

First angle orthographic drawings of the paper punch in the photograph are shown.

Draw to a scale of full size on A2 paper the following views:

1. The half section plan and the end elevation as shown. Use your own discretion where dimensions are missing. Show all the hidden edges (thickness of all metal 2mm).
2. A sectional front elevation, the plane of the section and the direction of the view being indicated by cutting plane B – B.
3. The true shape of the handle between E – F.

Add six important dimensions to your drawing and print a title block.

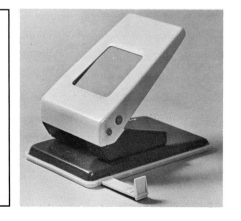

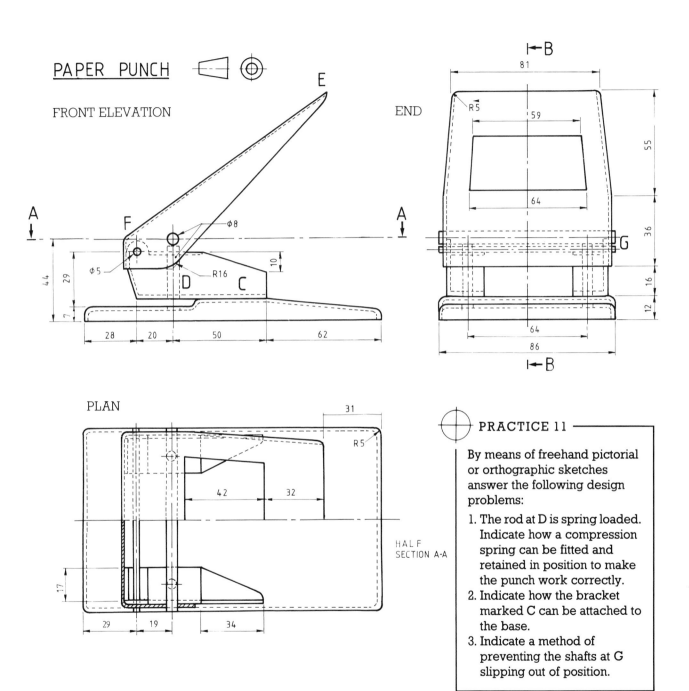

PAPER PUNCH

FRONT ELEVATION

END

PLAN

HALF
SECTION A-A

⊕ PRACTICE 11

By means of freehand pictorial
or orthographic sketches
answer the following design
problems:

1. The rod at D is spring loaded.
   Indicate how a compression
   spring can be fitted and
   retained in position to make
   the punch work correctly.
2. Indicate how the bracket
   marked C can be attached to
   the base.
3. Indicate a method of
   preventing the shafts at G
   slipping out of position.

# Freehand sketching: design problems

### PRACTICE 1

The photograph shows a vice for a milling machine. By means of freehand sketches, design a suitable winding handle which will fit on the end of the square section shaft. The handle is to be removable and you should produce more than one idea.

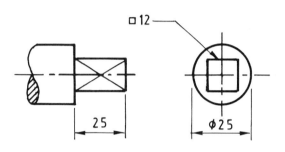

### PRACTICE 2

The photograph shows a drawer of a traditional sideboard.

By means of freehand pictorial sketches, design a knob or handle for the perspex door of a modern hi-fi cabinet. Use shading in your answer. More than one idea should be produced. State the materials from which the knob is to be made.

## PRACTICE 3

The photograph shows a tool rest for a wood turning lathe. The rest is tightened in position by rotating the handle as indicated by the arrow.

The drawing shows a section through the lathe bed with part of the body of the tool rest in position. When the handle is rotated the clamping piece is caused to move upwards as shown by the arrow. By means of freehand sketches, devise a mechanism which will convert the rotating movement of the handle to vertical movement of the clamp. (The clamp can be modified).

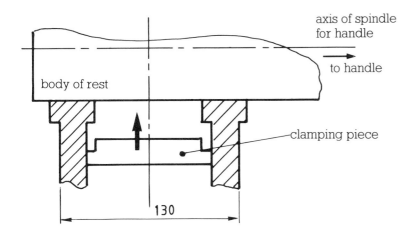

axis of spindle
for handle

to handle

body of rest

clamping piece

130

## PRACTICE 4

The photograph shows a door closer. The length of part AB can be adjusted. The actual adjusting device has been hidden.

By means of freehand sketches, design an adjuster for part AB. The adjustment should be continuous for 75mm.

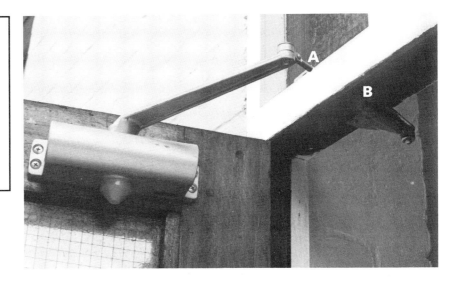

# Index